Faith With its Sleeves Rolled Up

Faith With its Sleeves Rolled Up

A collection of essays on the role of
faith in society

Edited by Daniel Singleton

First published in 2013
Copyright © 2013 FaithAction
ISBN 978-1-291-38891-6

Editorial assistance, layout and typesetting: Jeremy Simmons
Cover design by LifeLine Design
Cover photograph by Martin Smith Photography

www.faithaction.net

Printed and bound by Lulu

Contents

Contributors   vii
Introduction
    Daniel Singleton   1

Faith in Politics
    Stephen Timms   9

Faith and Muslims in Public Policy
    Daniel Nilsson DeHanas, Therese O'Toole and Nasar Meer   19

Attending to the Spirit in Mental Health
    Peter Gilbert   37

Faith and Looking After the Elderly
    Seeta Lakhani   53

Faith, Values and Community Well-being
    Sonia Douek   63

Faith Regen Foundation and Public Service Delivery
    Dr Husna Ahmad   77

Changing Shape, Keeping Vision
    Avril McIntyre   87

A Citizen's Right to Shape the Public Imagination
    Raheel Mohammed   97

**Forged in the Fires of Belief: An Exploration of Faith and
    Volunteering in Attend**
    David Wood   105

Could There Be Treasures in Our Faith? The Recognition and Utilisation of Spiritual Capital Values
Charles Oham   123

A Biblical Theology for Engaging With Society
Hugh Osgood   131

Speed & Scale
Matt Bird   145

Social Innovation and Enterprise as a Ground of the Common Good: The New Inter-Religious Frontier
Francis Davis   153

Contributors

Daniel Singleton is the National Executive Director of FaithAction and has worked at the forefront of faith-based innovative community projects for over 10 years. Initially working for a young charity in east London in the areas of adult and youth education and employability, Daniel now supports the work of organisations throughout the UK with public speaking, training and bespoke one-to-one consultancy.

Dr. Daniel Nilsson DeHanas is a Research Fellow in Sociology at the University of Kent. He has published research on issues including the "Olympics mega-mosque" controversy in Newham, young Muslim identities in Tower Hamlets and British Jamaican hip hop in Brixton. From 2010-12 he served as the research associate on the Muslim Participation in Contemporary Governance project at the University of Bristol.

Dr. Therese O'Toole is Senior Lecturer in Sociology at the University of Bristol. She is Principal Investigator on the Muslim Participation in Contemporary Governance project. She also leads Public Spirit, a new online forum on faith and public policy (www.publicspirit.org.uk). Her latest book is *Political Engagement amongst Ethnic Minority Young People: Making a Difference* (forthcoming 2013, with Richard Gale).

Dr. Nasar Meer is a Reader in Social Sciences and co-director of the Centre for Civil Society and Citizenship, Northumbria University.

Stephen Timms is the Member of Parliament for East Ham and the Shadow Minister for Employment. He is also the Labour Party's Faith Envoy. Stephen entered Parliament in 1994 and held a number of ministerial posts under the previous Labour Government including Chief Secretary to the Treasury and Financial Secretary to the Treasury. Before entering Parliament, Stephen worked in the telecommunications industry for fifteen years. He is a member of the Ramblers Association and Chair of the Christian Socialist Movement.

Peter Gilbert is Emeritus Professor of Social Work and Spirituality, Staffordshire University, and Associate Fellow in Education and Development, University of Warwick. He is the Project Lead for the National Spirituality and Mental Health Forum, and Editor of *Spirituality and Mental Health* (2011).

Seeta Lakhani runs Peepal Care, a domiciliary care agency in London. She studied Anthropology at UCL and has written two textbooks on Hinduism aimed at Key Stages 1-4. She also provides intercultural tours at the Victoria and Albert Museum on South Asian art and culture.

Sonia Douek is the Head of Volunteering and Community Development at Jewish Care, the largest health and social care provider to the UK Jewish community. She has been instrumental in introducing a strategy for volunteering that identifies best practice in the recruitment and support of almost 3,000 volunteers. Most recently she was the co-author of an "Agenda for Ageing Well in the Jewish Community," a call to action to ensure that older people feel connected and empowered to continue to be active members of their community.

Dr. Husna Ahmad OBE is the Group CEO of the Faith Regen Foundation, a Muslim-inspired multi faith charity working to empower disadvantaged communities in the UK and abroad. She is also the Secretary General of the World Muslim Leadership Forum. She is of Bangladeshi origin and has six children. Her particular interests are in environmental issues, engagement of faith communities in society and women's issues.

Avril McIntyre MBE has been Chief Executive of LifeLine Community Projects since its inception in 2000, and has taken creative ideas from the drawing board to inception with a focus on performance, growth and sustainability. LifeLine has developed a suite of services which engage some of the hardest to reach communities across London.

Raheel Mohammed is the founder and director of Maslaha and has recently been profiled as one of Britain's 50 New Radicals in *The Observer* newspaper for pioneering creative change to some of society's most difficult issues. Under his leadership Maslaha's work with Muslim communities and in the areas of health, education, culture and identity, and social entrepreneurship, has been actively used nationally and internationally. He has helped to set up other pioneering social enterprises and has been an award-winning journalist.

David Wood OBE is the Chief Executive of Attend, formerly the National Association of Hospital and Community Friends. Prior to this he was a Director of an Adult and Children's hospice in Essex. At the Department of Health, he is a member of the National Strategic Partnership Forum and the National Leadership Network. In 2010, David was appointed a Fellow of the Clore Social Leadership Programme, and also a Fellow of the NHS Institute for Innovation and Improvement. This year David has been seconded to Conservative Central Office.

Charles Oham is a Senior Lecturer in Social Enterprise at the School of Health and Social Care of the University of Greenwich. He is also a social enterprise trainer and practitioner.

Hugh Osgood is the chair of "Action in Communities," a church-related charity which modelled Christian work on multi-faith refugee settlement in the UK. He is also co-chair of the UK Charismatic and Pentecostal Leaders' Conference, and President of Churches in Communities International, the network for independent churches, ministries and networks. He holds a PhD on African and UK evangelical relationships from SOAS, University of London.

Matt Bird is the creator of Relationology, which is dedicated to analysing the art and science of relationships and how they drive business success. He is a provider of specialist motivational, training and consulting services (www.relationology.co.uk). He is also the voluntary Chair of The Cinnamon Network which is passionate about strengthening the muscles of local churches for community transformation (www.cinnamonnetwork.co.uk).

Francis Davis is an academic, journalist and social entrepreneur who has taught social enterprise and community development at the universities of Oxford and Cambridge. He is Visiting Fellow in Civic Innovation and Enterprise at Portsmouth University Business School.

Introduction
Daniel Singleton

In many ways, this is the right time to further the discussion of the value of faith to wider society. It is in the context of economic struggles and societal change, both of which are putting pressure on British people, that an examination of the contribution of faith is so important. And it is the activity of faith which motivates many of the contributors to this collection. Speaking for myself (and I am sure our contributors would agree with me) I dispute the idea that faith should be a private thing, as it forms the very essence of who I am. Faith gives us a reason to be, and provides a hope that motivates us to act in a way which does not put ourselves first. As such, people of faith make an important contribution to society, and in particular areas they are the lead contributors. In youth work, for instance, faith-based – and, in particular, Christian – work far outstrips that done by any other section of society, including the state.

When Stephen Timms launched the All Party Parliamentary Group (APPG) on Faith and Society in 2012 he used a quote by Christopher Hitchens as a springboard for discussion:

> [Faith organisations] don't prove any point and some of them are only making up for damage done ... they do involve a lot of proselytising, a lot of propaganda. They're not just giving out free stuff.[1]

The work of faith organisations, contrary to what this quote suggests, is not an excuse for winning converts; indeed, faith groups actively contribute to society, sometimes implicitly and sometimes explicitly, sometimes seen but often not. In fact, I believe that, when seeking to offer a helping hand with the problems faced by the world today, people of faith are often *"first in and last out."* This book looks at some examples of this contribution, but it only scratches the surface. It is not a list of answers, or a manifesto, but a conversation starter, and therefore sits

---

[1] George Eaton, "Preview II: Richard Dawkins interviews Christopher Hitchens," in *The new Statesman*, accessed April 2013, http://www.newstatesman.com/blogs/the-staggers/2011/12/christopher-hitchens-evening?quicktabs_most_read=1.

neatly alongside the work of the APPG, which was set up to examine the contribution that faith brings to society and the ways in which these benefits can be shared, improved upon and magnified. This book, we hope, will be of interest not only to policy shapers, commissioners and funders but also to the faith communities themselves. As Jay Lakhani of the Hindu Academy said, "Faith is not merely about going to the temples and collecting coconuts." At the London Mayor's conference on interfaith in February 2011, Boris Johnson threw down a similar challenge to those present by quoting from the letter of James in the New Testament: "faith by itself, if it does not have works, is dead."[2]

It is this purposeful, engaged faith that forms the focus of this book. Faith that is ready to get involved, that has its *sleeves rolled up*, we argue, can be of great benefit both to faith communities and society as a whole. There are some who would say, contrary to this, that in order to preserve its distinctiveness faith should take a step back from the problems faced by wider society (an attitude reminiscent, perhaps, of that which led to the creation of religious "ghettos" throughout history). Of course, it is important for faith groups to be distinctive, but this does not mean they should neglect to offer a helping hand. A balance should be struck whereby faith groups are able to make a difference whilst retaining the ethos and values that make them unique. Unfortunately, however, finding this balance is can often be difficult. As the APPG has taken evidence from various faith groups, there has been a consistent perception that, although commissioners and funders appreciate – and, in some ways, marvel at – faith-based initiatives, the groups themselves often feel under pressure to make light of or even conceal their faith ethos, the very thing which makes them who they are and which undergirds their work.

My role with FaithAction gives me the opportunity to speak with many different people about faith and its role in twenty-first-century UK society, both adherents to faith and those on the outside. There are a number of key roles for faith communities, institutions and faith-based organisations (FBOs) which come up as part of these conversations, and a number of them are picked up by the contributors to this book. As we look at these different roles below, bear in mind that many of them overlap and interact.

---

[2] James 2:14-26 (New King James Version).

Solution-focused innovation

It is often the case that FBOs find themselves dealing with people and situations that have been overlooked. Unable to just complain and advocate, although this is part of the role, FBOs look to intervene. Sometimes with an off-the-shelf community franchise, but more often than not with a bespoke response which is then developed into something more sophisticated as time goes on. Much of what faith groups do could be described as relief work, but there is also innovation and enterprise, borne out of a real understanding of the situation on the ground and access to the insight and expertise of faith communities, which can be channeled to produce a lasting solution and sometimes address the underlying cause.

Connectedness, neighbourliness and identity

There are many new, innovative ideas to come from faith groups, then, but connectedness of community is something they have been practicing for a long time. Time and again, we hear of the broken nature of British society, yet faith groups often make up communities within communities, providing intergenerational opportunities unrivalled beyond the football stadium. Essentially, what we have is extended family. There is identity, sharing and service against the backdrop of an individualist, consumerist society. Faith is shown to strengthen families and marriages and to keep young people in positive peer groups and away from the false family and belonging of gangs.

Engagement, involvement and mobilisation

When I speak to people of faith about their acts of service, it is interesting to note that many of them feel that what they are doing is ordinary when, in fact, it is very unusual. One only has to visit the Nishkam Centre in Birmingham, and hear about the way the community came together to build the community centre (in what amounted to 110,000 hours of work and £1.5m worth of volunteering) to be taken aback. On a personal note, my wife was very ill after the birth of one of our children, for a period of time she was even in a wheelchair, but our church community rallied round providing a hot meal every day for the whole family for a number of months, as well as extra child care. When this service spills out of the faith community to the wider community we can see what mobilised faith can really achieve. It is the unsung volunteer army at the base of faith communities that provides such potential. Mobilised faith involves not only straightforward activities like litter picking, but also the more specialised work of professionals and tradesmen within congregations, using their skills to mentor and aid others.

A focus on the whole

It is this focus on the "person" (people and church workers) rather than the "plant" (fixed and moveable assets) that led one group of Christians to describe church as "not so much a building but more a way of life." Where the public and private sectors continually treat people as a collection of parts, those of faith see people as whole beings: body, mind and spirit, a point that Peter Gilbert expands on in his chapter. Yet if real lasting solutions are to be found for the ills of society we will have to address the whole person.

A source of hope

As Stephen Timms outlines in his chapter, faith and politics are both about hope for the future, about vision and values. There is a role for faith to play in holding our leaders to account and encouraging them to lead rather than respond simply to the lowest common denominator of perceived public opinion. Even in a literary sense, scripture can provide a greater source for political rhetoric than pop culture, references to which seem to frequently work their way into the interactions of politicians. Yet the longevity of faith and its absolute doctrine mean that people of faith are not shaped by the whims of society's taste, but are encouraged to do right and act well even if unappreciated. The values and sense of hope that faith provides to many in key positions in society are important for the fast moving world we live in.

The chapters to follow are diverse in their exploration of the wide-reaching significance of faith ideas. We begin with Stephen Timms' own experiences both as a Christian and an MP. Drawing on his ten years in government, Stephen Timms looks to challenge the assumption that faith and politics do not and should not mix, arguing instead that "faith is a great starting points for politics, one of the best starting points there is." In highlighting the core values that underlie faith traditions, he puts forward the case that these values might act as a solid foundation for a compassionate politics.

Sticking with politics, Daniel DeHanas, Therese O'Toole and Nasar Meer chart, in their chapter, the development of a "faith paradigm" in public policy, tracing its emergence back to the latter half of the 1980s. In the light of this history, the writers analyse the differences between New Labour's approach to faith and that of the current Coalition government, asking whether David Cameron's label "a Christian country" is indeed a useful one in describing the nature of British religious life today.

Echoing Stephen Timms' addressing of the tricky relationship between faith and politics, Peter Gilbert sets out to challenge the popular opinion that there is something of a "standoff," too, between the worlds of faith and science, referencing, in particular, the role faith might play in health and social care. In fact, says Gilbert, acknowledgement of the "spiritual" needs of care recipients can be a vital key to recovery, providing patients with not only a "framework for life" and value base, but also a sense of community and mutual obligation.

Seeta Lakhani's experience in providing care for the elderly also makes clear the value of acknowledging the "spiritual," as she writes about the vital role that faith can play in domiciliary care. The "faith-sensitive care" she describes recognises the importance of spiritual matters for people in their later years, acknowledging, too, that faith's emphasis on community and family values can help combat the isolation often felt by elderly people, reconnecting these individuals with positive social networks.

Sonia Douek provides a further challenge in considering how we might engage with older members of society within the broader context of "community wellbeing." If wellbeing hinges on working productively and making a contribution to one's community, why then, asks Douek, are the elderly so often pushed to the fringes and treated simply as care recipients? The Jewish concept of "tzedakah," she argues, provides an alternative model, going further than one-way support and communicating the belief that true giving should also be empowering.

As Husna Ahmad explains in her chapter, Faith Regen Foundation, a Muslim-inspired, multi-faith organisation, is similarly committed to going beyond "charity" and equipping those reached: poverty alleviation in Islam, she says, "is about investment, education and lifting people out of impoverishment." Indeed, a similar commitment can be located in Avril McIntyre's chapter, which charts the development of LifeLine Projects, an East-London-based social enterprise. Together, McIntyre and Dr Ahmad's contributions offer valuable insight into the journeys of grassroots enterprises devoted to the task of putting faith into action. Their paths have not been free of obstacles, however; a number of difficult questions have been raised along the way. How, to name one, could Faith Regen successfully meet government contracts whilst staying true to its founding faith values? And how would LifeLine preserve its "solution-focused" ethos amid rapid growth and changes to personnel? Both writers reflect thoughtfully on the way forward for faith-inspired enterprises committed to supporting the vulnerable and building community.

Drawing inspiration from centuries of cultural history, Raheel Mohammad paints a vivid picture of the power of both religion and art to shape public imagination and, in turn, inspire social change. Mohammad's charity, Maslaha, another faith-based social enterprise, is dedicated to the "widening of language" around the health and social issues we face today. Maslaha harnesses the power of metaphor, via interactive workshops and art exhibitions, to challenge assumptions and draft a vision for the future.

The work of social enterprises like Faith Regen, LifeLine and Maslaha, as well as charities like Feepal Care and Jewish Care, is so often underpinned by the efforts of volunteers, a subject addressed by David Wood. As Chief Executive of Attend, Wood has long wondered about the motivations of the individuals that give their time to Attend's member organisations. Conducting ten interviews with volunteers up and down the country, he found that, alongside faith and other motivations, altruism plays a considerable part in encouraging people to volunteer – a conclusion apparently at odds with prevailing contemporary opinion. A sample of three of Wood's interviews is included, here.

Charles Oham sheds further light on the motivations behind enterprise; in his chapter, he proposes a looser understanding of the term "social entrepreneurship," acknowledging that there are a wide variety of reasons, alongside the "social," why people choose to trade for charitable purposes. A spiritual motivation is key among these, he says, and the value it adds has come to be termed "spiritual capital." Oham unpacks this concept and highlights the benefits it brings to the enterprise table, among them an increased capacity for social innovation as well as an encouragement towards sustainability and stewardship of resources. Unlocking the potential of spiritual capital is vital, says Oham, for addressing the pressing social and environmental issues of our time.

That people of faith ought to do things like address social issues and shape culture has been taken for granted in the chapters presented so far; Hugh Osgood responds, in his, to those who believe the Christian Church should step back. Osgood argues, instead, that being in relationship with God should inspire "a whole-hearted and generous engagement with the surrounding society." He identifies and confutes two historical misunderstandings of the Church's relationship to society, domination and detachment, outlining, in their place, a biblical interpretation of the Church as a "community within a community," a group of people responding to the world's problems from a position of love.

So how might Christians quickly, effectively and lovingly address the increasing social need within our communities? Matt Bird proposes a solution in the form of "community franchising." His chapter outlines the activities of the Cinnamon Network in helping replicate the transformative social projects of local Christian churches on a national scale. Where thriving projects already exist, the Network helps transfer their successes to other pockets of need, thus enabling churches to rediscover their capacity for voluntary action and community transformation.

Picking up the theme of social innovation among faith-based groups, Francis Davis' chapter echoes Matt Bird's call for new ideas in answer to the fragmentary nature of contemporary culture. Lack of willingness within faith communities to accurately measure achievements, combined with a breakdown in communication due to ambiguous terminology, has meant that the actions of faith groups have been largely undervalued in recent years. This situation might be changed, says Davis, through the implementation of "social silicon valleys," or faith-based social innovation hubs. Such "valleys" would enable faith-inspired ideas to be developed, mobilised and measured, opening the door to new strategies of "knowledge transfer" among faith institutions that might begin to shape culture for the good.

Faith's capacity to positively influence culture in this way means it should not be shuffled off to one particular policy area or government department. Faith is not a problem for which to form a contingency, or merely a way of reaching people who are less connected to services. Faith is a route to many possibilities and people. Society is at a loss if it does not recognise and make use of the presence of faith, and I hope that the chapters to follow will demonstrate how faith might positively interact with society, changing it for the better.

I would like to extend my thanks, first, to all of our contributors. There are a number of people whose input has been key to this project, but the most significant behind-the-scenes contribution came from Jeremy Simmons, who took on much of the legwork in putting the book together. Fresh out of university, Jeremy went above and beyond to facilitate its publication. Of course, there are many others in the background – family, friends and colleagues – who have assisted our work at FaithAction, but I would like to give special mention to Felicity Smith, Hannah Walker, Alan Fitch and Chris Miller, as the other members of the FaithAction team who have assisted along the way and helped make this happen.

Daniel Singleton, London, April 2013.

Faith in Politics
Stephen Timms

A lot of people say you shouldn't mix up faith and politics. It's not hard to make a persuasive case. Point out problems in some part of the world where the protagonists have clear faith positions – Belfast, Baghdad or Bombay, for example – and the argument is made.

But I don't agree with the argument. On the contrary, my argument is the reverse. It seems to me that faith is a great starting point for politics, one of the best starting points there is. Because faith is a source of exactly the values we need to make politics work.

Faith and politics are both about hope. Faith provides a basis for hope that things will be put right in the future. Politicians also, if they are to gain support, have to inspire hope for a better future. To some extent, because both are dealing with hope – albeit in rather different terms – they may sometimes step on each other's toes. But their shared pre-occupation with hope also gives them something important in common. Language and ways of speaking developed in a context of faith can often prove effective in political communication too. It is striking how often, for example, in supposedly secular Britain, that language used successfully by New Labour to explain its political message had its roots in the New Testament.

Renewing the values that can make politics work

Faith is a great source of values: responsibility, solidarity, persistence, patience, compassion, truthfulness. They are exactly the values which can make democratic politics work. If those values are eroded then politics no longer works as well – and that is one of the reasons, in my view, for current disenchantment with politics. We need new sources for reinvigorating adherence to those values, and the faith communities can help us. It is not clear that other institutions or movements have as much to offer.

The think tank Demos produced a report called *Faithful Citizens: why those who do God, do good*.[1] They looked at evidence from the respected European Values Survey, and found that one in eight of the UK population say they belong to a religious organisation. And then they looked at evidence from the survey about who the active citizens are.

They found that the proportion who have volunteered for local community action is 6% among those who belong to a religious organisation, compared with 1% among those who don't. That is, committed religious people are six times more likely to be active citizens in their community than those who don't belong to a religious organisation.

The number who have volunteered in youth work is 11% among those who belong to a religious organisation, compared with just 3% among those who don't. The proportion who have volunteered on development or human rights issues is 4% among those who belong to a religious organisation, compared with half a percent among those who don't. In fact, on this, and on the number working on women's issues or for a trade union, the one in eight who belong to a religious organisation account for more volunteers than the seven in eight who don't.

The evidence indicates that people who belong to religious organisations are more likely than others to be good citizens. And, when they come together to argue for political change, we get exactly the kind of idealistic, popular movement which can inspire successful politics. That is, politics which can inspire and engage, can provide people with fresh hope, and give a basis for positive political change. That is what happened in the church-led campaign to abolish the slave trade two centuries ago; and in the formation and growth of the labour movement and Labour Party from the network of chapels and trade union branches among working people a century ago; and more recently in the *Jubilee 2000* and *Make Poverty History* campaigns, in which 80% of the supporters who turned up on human chains and other demonstrations – the people who gave the campaigns their energy and their effectiveness – came from the churches.

It's happening again in the current campaigns of *London Citizens* for a living wage and for safe places for young people. London Citizens is a

[1] Jonathan Birdwell and Mark Littler, "Faithful Citizens: Why those who do God, do good," a report for Demos, April 2012.

remarkable coalition drawn from churches, mosques, synagogues, schools, trade union branches and community organisations. It is having a striking, positive impact on a broad range of politicians and companies.

There can be no better foundation than movements of this kind for renewing our politics. People with firm faith commitments have often been reluctant to become entangled with party politics, for fear of finding themselves with conflicting loyalties. Those who have taken the plunge have not always been made welcome. In my view, that needs to change.

Faith and cohesion

The above argument may have been viable, some may suggest, in an era in Britain when it could be assumed that people of faith would all be Christians. But over a third of my constituents are Muslims, and Britain has large Jewish, Hindu and Sikh communities. Is it not inevitable that different faith groups, far from building cohesive civic politics, will, if they become politically active, provoke divisions?

It is important to address this widely held concern. It is worth starting by pointing out that British communities have not been homogeneous in faith terms for hundreds of years. It is true that the numerous places of worship in a Victorian English town will all have been Christian, but there were sharp and keenly felt differences between them. In most places, this does not appear to have weakened the cohesiveness of the community.

It seems to me that fragmentation, or the breakdown of cohesion, does not occur when people belong to lots of different things, so long as it is clear that the different things are all part of the wider community. The problem arises when people don't belong to anything at all. The community I represent includes dozens of churches, mosques and temples, which do all see themselves as part of the wider community. It is marked by a high degree of belonging – and therefore, it seems to me, by a high degree of cohesion, rather than by the fragmentation which pessimists might assume would follow. Communities with much less faith diversity, but also much less belonging, are more fragmented and less cohesive. So I see faith diversity as a foundation for civic cohesion rather than for division.

When London's bid for the 2012 Olympics was being considered by the International Olympic Committee in Singapore in 2005, some forty schoolchildren from East London went to show what modern London is like. They were lively and enthusiastic. They had family roots in every different part of the world, but they were proud of the city which was home to all of them. They presented an optimistic vision of how the world might be in the future, and they were important in securing support for the London bid.

The Opening Ceremony for the London Games, on 27 July 2012, successfully captured that optimistic view of the future for a multi-cultural society, where different faith backgrounds are respected, but people are bound together by shared pride in their nation and by trust in institutions like the National Health Service. Politics needs to capture that spirit of civic commitment as well, and engaging with and learning from the faith communities is an important way to do it.

A multi-cultural constituency

I had always been interested in politics, but, as a student in the 1970s, all my spare time was spent in my college Christian Union. One summer, we went to help out on a church mission in Forest Gate, in the east London Borough of Newham which I now represent in the House of Commons. It was only a fortnight, but when it finished I was hooked. I left college in late 1978, started a job in London with a software company, and went to live in Newham. I joined the church which had by then been planted by the mission team, and I am still a member. And I joined the Labour Party.

Newham was already then clearly a multi-racial borough. It had hosted a Jewish community for a century, and West Indians had made their homes in Newham since the 1950s. In 1972, when Idi Amin expelled Asians from Uganda, many came to Newham. Others, with roots in South India and employed by the British forces in Singapore, came to East London when the British military left. Our mission team, in 1976, used Patrick Sookhdeo's booklet *Asians in Britain*.

I was unsure how an enthusiastic Christian Union member like me would be viewed in this multi-racial, and multi-religious, area. I became a local Councillor in 1984, and started to find that I related well to people with faith commitments that were firm, but different to mine. I became Chair of the Council's planning committee in 1987. I was on the receiving end of a march to the Town Hall by demonstrators from the Alliance of Newham Muslim Associations, led by Ahmed Din, Chair of the Alliance and local businessman, and Yusuf Islam, the former pop star Cat Stevens. They were carrying a coffin and demanding space in the area where Muslim burials could be carried out. At the time, bodies were often flown back to Pakistan for burial.

It struck me that it was in fact in the interests of everyone that people who had lived in our community should be able to be buried decently in our community. And we agreed that an area of the Council's own cemetery would be laid out for Muslim burials, the graves pointing towards Mecca.

In 1990 I was elected Leader of Newham Council. In 1994, our MP, Ron Leighton, died suddenly and unexpectedly from a heart attack. We needed to select a candidate to replace him. Ahmed Din rang me up. He said they felt I should seek the nomination. "You believe in God. We believe in God." was his argument. I was selected, and won the by-election which followed. Being a person of faith was an important part of the reason for my selection by the Labour Party as its candidate. And I have had a very strong vested interest ever since in arguing that people with firm, but different, faith commitments can work together successfully in politics.

I joined the opposition backbenches in June 1994. In May 1997, when Labour won a landslide victory under Tony Blair, I was appointed a Parliamentary Private Secretary. A year later I became a Minister in the Department for Social Security, and held ministerial office for the next twelve years. I was a Minister in the Treasury on four separate occasions, which I believe is probably some kind of record. In 2006-7, I served in Tony Blair's last Cabinet as Chief Secretary to the Treasury. I was pensions minister twice, business minister three times and schools minister for a year. I was employment minister in 2008, a role which I currently shadow on the Opposition front bench.

I am sometimes asked whether faith has helped or hindered my political career. I have explained that it helped me be selected as a parliamentary candidate in the first place. I cannot recall any occasion when I felt that I was being held back because someone objected to my faith. On the other hand, being an active Christian probably meant that I spent my time in ways not best designed to secure a high-flying political career. I have never been particularly clubbable. My Cabinet career was short – I was not reappointed when Gordon Brown took over from Tony Blair, although Gordon was careful to appoint me to a junior ministerial role I was interested in.

On balance, my view is that being a person of faith has contributed more to advancing my political career than to holding it back. I will leave the reader to decide whether that is a good or a bad thing.

Delivering compassion

In 2008, I was appointed Financial Secretary to the Treasury, responsible for the Government's policy on taxation. The financial crisis was just breaking. I attended the G20 summit in London in April 2009, when countries were struggling with a sharp drop in tax revenues in the wake of the crisis, and there was a lot of concern about tax avoidance.

Soon afterwards, I met at their request with representatives from Christian Aid, who wanted to argue for "country by country reporting." They produced a pamphlet setting out theological arguments for their case.[2] What they meant was that multinational companies should be required to report each year the profit which they earn, and the tax which they pay, in each country where they operate. In that way it would become obvious where companies were using accounting devices to hide their profits in low tax jurisdictions, and so avoiding tax which would otherwise be owed to developing countries. The scale of this type of – perfectly legal – tax avoidance is immense, and developing countries' tax revenues are much lower than they might be as a result. Their need for aid is therefore much higher than it would be if all the tax due was paid.

When the Christian Aid representatives had left, I asked the Treasury officials at the meeting what they thought. They agreed that Christian Aid had a point, and that opaqueness in multinationals' tax payments was a problem. We agreed I would promote a discussion of this idea of "country by country reporting."

---

[2] Paul Clifford and Angus Ritchie. "The Gospel and the Rich: theological views of tax," *Christian Aid*, London, June 2009.

In July, I raised the topic at a meeting of European tax ministers. Gordon Brown, the Prime Minister, picked up what I was doing and raised it with French President Nicolas Sarkozy at the Anglo-French summit at the end of July. From there it came to the attention of the OECD. A special joint meeting of the OECD's tax and development committees was convened in Paris in January 2010. Country by country reporting was a major point on the agenda, and it was agreed that the idea should be worked up into one of the OECD's guidelines for good practice on the part of multi-national companies.

My work at the Treasury came to an end at the General Election in May 2010, but the idea of country by country reporting has continued to gain support. Christian Aid, together with Action Aid and Oxfam, have continued to give it strong backing. It featured unexpectedly in legislation passed by the US Congress, and signed by President Barack Obama in Summer 2010. And, more recently, it has been the subject of legislation in the European Parliament too.

I would like to see more of that: people starting from a faith viewpoint realising that change is needed, and lobbying politicians to implement the change. It can take some time, rather than happening quickly. But it means that change can be rooted in the values shared by faith communities – and, in time, wider confidence in politics can be renewed as a result.

I have already mentioned the Jubilee 2000 and Make Poverty History campaigns, which were larger scale examples of political change being inspired by insights and commitment drawn from faith. Government support for the fair trade movement is another example.

Faith communities' inspiration of policies does not need to be limited to international development. There is substantial potential for renewing policy on domestic matters too.

Faith and unemployment

Faith groups have long been troubled by unemployment. William Booth, founder of the Salvation Army, established the first unemployment exchange. In 1997, the report drawn up by the Council of Churches of Britain and Ireland on *Unemployment and the Future of Work* set out the basic moral case that "it is wrong, in so prosperous a society as ours, for large numbers of men and women to be deprived for long periods of the means to earn a living." That thinking was carried forward in the New Deal programme introduced by the Labour Government which was elected shortly after the report was published.

Numerous church-based initiatives participated in the New Deal, and have continued to support jobseekers into work since. In London, I have seen the effective work of Pecan in Peckham, with a speciality among ex-offenders; of Spear, drawing on the congregation of St Paul's Hammersmith to mentor young people into work; of City Gateway in East London, rooted in Christian faith and serving Bangladeshi women among others. Faith Regen is a Muslim-led charity which is working as a sub-contractor on the Government's Work Programme. I recently visited two church-based job clubs in Devon – at Axminster Methodist Church and at Glenorchy United Reformed Church at Exmouth, which was celebrating its first anniversary. Both are replacing, to some extent, official local jobcentres which had been closed down. At Exmouth, one of those present took me to one side to emphasise that, for her, the job club had been literally a lifeline.

All these initiatives bring together people motivated by their faith, whether volunteers or paid workers, who are interested in the individuals they are seeking to help. They will plug away, even if, at times, an observer might feel they are wasting their time. The jobseekers can get to know them, over an extended period if necessary, and draw consistently on their support. At Axminster, a regular attender explained to me that his job club helper had enabled him to obtain an email address for the first time, and shown him how to search for jobs online. Conventional jobcentres – struggling with staffing cuts and large numbers of unemployed people – simply can't do that. The idea in New Deal that jobcentre advisers would get to know their clients has long since been abandoned; in the latest version of "fast sign on," there is no conversation at all.

And, to be successful, politics needs to be able to draw inspiration from the imperative which those projects are living out: inspired by commitment to help individual jobseekers, acknowledging the importance of reducing the scale of unemployment and determined to implement economic policies which can provide hope to people worn down by disappointments.

The experience of welfare to work projects in Australia has been very influential on thinking in the UK. In Australia, the market-leading welfare to work provider is the Salvation Army. The second biggest provider is Mission Australia – a descendant of a nineteenth-century operation established by the London City Mission. UK policy needs to recognise the value of the contribution of faith-based initiatives too.

A politics of shared values

Too often, politics treats faith as irrelevant, or embarrassing, or even dangerous. Politicians are polite but dismissive. I have set out in this chapter some examples when politicians have taken their lead from the faith communities. We need more of those in the future. They lead to policies which are genuinely rooted in the experiences of communities, reflecting values which are widely shared. This is the kind of politics which can enthuse and engage people – including people who have no interest in faith at all.

It is important, however, to recognise that a large proportion of the UK population ally themselves with one or other of the faith communities. I quoted above the statistic from the European Values Survey: one in eight of the UK population belongs to a religious organisation. As I write the data on religion from the 2011 census has not yet been published, but in the 2001 census 75% of the population answered the voluntary question about faith by associating themselves with one of the major faiths, 72% with Christianity and 3% with one of the others.

And the old assumption that faith participation has been declining appears no longer to be true – at least not in the major cities. The electoral roll of the Church of England diocese of London fell steadily from 1972 to 1992, but has risen equally steadily in the twenty years since – and is now back where it was 40 years ago, and still growing. And today's enormous African churches, mosques and temples, entirely outside these statistics, were undreamt of 40 years ago. The importance of these trends on our communities, and their importance for our politics, can only grow in the years ahead.

Some dialogues with faith communities over policy will be harder than the examples I have set out here. For example, the Prime Minister's proposal for changing the definition of marriage to include gay unions has been widely supported across the House of Commons. It has, however, been firmly opposed by the Church of England, the Roman Catholic Church, the Muslim Council of Britain and the Chief Rabbi. It would be a mistake, in my view, simply to dismiss their objections out of hand as obscurantist homophobia. There needs at least to be a proper dialogue, and a serious effort to understand why the faith communities have taken the view that they have. The Government's consultation has certainly not delivered that so far.

Faith and politics can be uncomfortable associates. But the effort needs to be made – and making it is one of the keys to a democratic politics which can succeed in the twenty-first century.

Faith and Muslims in Public Policy
Daniel Nilsson DeHanas, Therese O'Toole and Nasar Meer

"Faith" is an important – and often highly charged – topic in contemporary public policy. Many ministerial speeches and government policy documents incorporate positive language about "faith communities," "inter-faith work," and "faith-based social action," while others address darker themes such as "religious extremism" and "Islamophobia." This has not always been so. Previous research suggests that in the years leading into the mid-1990s policymakers considered faith a taboo subject that was difficult to even mention in public. In 1993, the Secretary of the Inner Cities Religious Council David Randolph-Horn gave a speech to raise awareness of a "faith paradigm." In his remarks he observed: "I think we find it easier to cope with a race paradigm."[1]

Times have changed. The "faith paradigm" that Randolph-Horn was promoting has gained prominence over the course of the 1990s and 2000s. Today "faith" arguably has as much if not more salience in policy circles than race or ethnicity.[2] In our research we have traced changes in three distinct, though overlapping, fields in which faith has emerged as significant. These three policy fields are:

1. *equality and diversity* (e.g., multiculturalism, community cohesion)

---

[1] Jenny Taylor "There's Life in the Establishment – But Not as We Know It," in *Political Theology*, Vol. 5, No. 3, 2004, p. 337. For more detail on the "secular" assumptions of government and governance in the 1990s, and how these made way for religious discourses, see Jenny Taylor (2002) "After Secularism: Inner-City Governance and the New Religious Discourse," unpublished PhD thesis. London: SOAS.

[2] For the transition from a politics of race to faith, see Tariq Modood (2005) *Multicultural Politics: Racism, Ethnicity and Muslims in Britain*. Edinburgh: Edinburgh University Press. See also Sean McLoughlin, "From Race to Faith Relations, the Local to the National Level: The State and Muslim Organisations in Britain," in A. Kreienbrink and M. Bodenstein, eds. (2010) *Muslim Organisations and the State: European Perspectives*. Nürnberg, Germany: Bundesamt für Migration und Flüchtlinge, pp. 123-149.

2. *faith sector governance* (referring to the role of faith and inter-faith groups in government partnerships, welfare delivery, and urban regeneration)

3. *security* (e.g., preventing violent extremism, border control)

The research study we have just completed[3] investigates the various roles Muslims have played in these three policy fields – as advisors, authors, innovators, targets, or critics of government policies. Muslim-government relations have changed considerably in the course of the past few decades, and the story of the emergence of a "faith paradigm" is inseparably also a story of Muslim participation in governance.

In this chapter we will describe some of the major developments in the emergence of a "faith paradigm" in British public policy. It is important to note that the focus of our research study on Muslim participation means that the chapter will not directly address the roles of various other religious traditions (such as Hindus or Baha'is) in these developments. The inclusion of Muslims and these other faiths in British policymaking and governance has always had some relationship to the Church of England, however, and therefore the Church does feature in our narrative here. The weak establishment of a national Church in England is frequently welcomed by leaders of Britain's diverse religious traditions, who see religious establishment as an inherent critique of strict secularism and as a facilitator of their inclusion.[4] Some have traced Britain's high degree of multicultural openness to different faiths (in comparison to other European countries) to this weak establishment tradition.[5] For these reasons, any change in the Church of England's relationship with government has far-reaching consequences for the

---

[3] This chapter is based on the research of the *Muslim Participation in Contemporary Governance* project at the University of Bristol, funded by the AHRC/ESRC Religion & Society Programme. From July 2010 to December 2012, the research team led by Dr Therese O'Toole completed an analysis of national and local government policies since 1997 and over 100 qualitative interviews with political, administrative, and Muslim civil society actors. The final report, *Taking Part: Muslim Participation in British Government, Policymaking and Governance*, will be published and available online on 31 January 2013. Further details on the project are available at:
http://www.bristol.ac.uk/ethnicity/projects/muslimparticipation/.
[4] Tariq Modood, ed. (1997) *Church, State and religious minorities. Vol. 845.* London: Policy Studies Institute.
[5] Nasar Meer and Tariq Modood. "Contemporary developments in cases of Muslim-state engagement," in A. Triandafyllidou, ed. (2010) *Muslims in 21st Century Europe: Structural and Cultural Perspectives.* Oxford: Routledge.

inclusion of other faiths, as will become apparent in our analysis that follows.

The growing visibility of faith groups: 1985-1997

Two key moments of vocal religious activism in the 1980s set the scene for coming developments in faith-related public policy. In 1985, the Archbishop of Canterbury's Commission on Urban Priority Areas published the report *Faith in the City*. It was a "collectivist" critique of the Thatcher government's policies on urban regeneration, setting out a vision of church action on urban poverty. *Faith in the City* resulted in the creation of the Church Urban Fund to better address poverty at a parish level. It also caused a substantial rift in relations between the Church and the government of the time, with an unnamed cabinet minister dismissing it as "pure Marxist theology."[6]

Religion took centre stage again in the Rushdie Affair of 1988-89. British Muslims who considered Salman Rushdie's novel *The Satanic Verses* to be a blasphemous misrepresentation of the Prophet Muhammad protested in large numbers across the country. Some formed the UK Action Committee on Islamic Affairs (UKACIA) to coordinate their collective action. Secretary of State for Education John Patten sent a letter to the leaders of UKACIA and other Muslim groups, in which he attempted to defuse the situation while suggesting that British Muslims improve their English and understanding of how democracy works.[7] Despite the patronising response from government, the Rushdie Affair had instilled Muslim activists with a newfound confidence. Indeed, it stood in contrast to the Honeyford Affair of 1984, in which campaigning for the recognition of Muslim practices at a Bradford school had been led by secular activists and anti-racists such as Jenny Woodward.[8]

---

[6] John Campbell (2003) *Margaret Thatcher: The Iron Lady*. London: Jonathan Cape, p. 390.

[7] Jamil Sherif, "A Census chronicle – reflections on the campaign for a religion question in the 2001 Census for England and Wales," in *Journal of Beliefs & Values: Studies in Religion & Education*, Vol. 32, No. 1, 2011, p. 16.

[8] The Honeyford Affair was a local controversy that received national media coverage. A Bradford school headmaster named Ray Honeyford opposed the implementation of cultural diversity policies, including the provision of Halal meals, adaptations of school uniforms and a multi-faith religious education curriculum. This sparked anti-racist campaigning for Muslim recognition. See Dervla Murphy (1987) *Tales from Two Cities: Travels of Another Sort*. London: Penguin, p. 110.

Faith in the City and the Rushdie Affair each demonstrated a growing assertiveness of faith actors in British public life. These dissenting religious voices from the 1980s began to formalise new relationships with the state in the 1990s, creating the Inner Cities Religious Council (ICRC) and the Muslim Council of Britain. The ICRC was a consultative body established in 1992 by the Archbishop of Canterbury and John Major's government, and initially based in the Department of the Environment. It was designed to be a mechanism by which faith groups could influence central government policies on urban regeneration. The ICRC was intended to "mend fences" between government and the Church of England in the wake of *Faith in the City*.[9]

Importantly, the ICRC was established not simply as an Anglican body but as one that was inclusive of the five largest British faith traditions (Christian, Hindu, Jewish, Muslim, and Sikh). This multi-faith approach was influenced by another significant faith organisation at that time, the Inter Faith Network for the UK (IFN). The IFN was founded in 1987 by Brian Pearce, who had taken a leave of absence from the civil service to investigate the health of inter-faith activity in the UK. In 1987 there were only 30 local inter-faith bodies in the UK. By the time of the IFN's 20th anniversary in 2007 there were more than 210 such bodies, due in large part to the IFN's own advocacy work.[10]

The Muslim Council of Britain became another important representative body at the national level. Iqbal Sacranie, a London businessman and a co-convener of the UKACIA steering group, was one of the two Muslim representatives on the ICRC. Sacranie's experience in the ICRC helped him to recognise the need for a national Muslim organisation with a broader remit than UKACIA. He was among the community leaders who, in Autumn 1994, fielded a national survey of Muslim needs under the auspices of the National Interim Committee on Muslim Unity (NICMU). The results of this survey and further consultations culminated in the founding of the Muslim Council of Britain (MCB) in November 1997 as a national umbrella body that brought many Muslim

---

[9] Interview with David Rayner, 16/10/2011.
[10] (2007) "The Inter Faith Network for the UK: 20 Years: Milestones on the Journey Together Towards Greater Inter Faith Understanding and Cooperation." London: The Inter Faith Network for the UK. In addition to the ICRC and IFN, another important national multi-faith body has been the Faith-based Regeneration Network (FbRN). The FbRN was set up in 2002 to facilitate cooperation between the nine largest UK faiths in regeneration and community development.

organisations together with a single voice.[11] Sacranie became its first Secretary General.

The emergence of a New Labour "faith" agenda: 1997-2001

New Labour's first term (1997-2001) ushered in a sea change of positive developments for Britain's diverse faith communities. State funding for faith schools was expanded beyond Christian and Jewish schools for the first time, enabling parity for Muslims, Sikhs, Hindus, and potentially others. A religion question was added to the 2001 Census in recognition of the importance of religion as a form of self-identification for many people. Faith played a role in national commemorations: Holocaust Memorial Day was introduced and the Lambeth Group incorporated faith into the Millennium celebrations.[12] Alongside these and other developments, the Muslim Council of Britain enjoyed insider status during these early years of the Blair government. It was frequently acknowledged in public events, invited to receptions, and regarded as a major interlocutor with government.[13]

Perhaps some of these developments in the public recognition of faith could have been expected. Several in the New Labour leadership, including Tony Blair and Jack Straw, had been active in the Christian Socialist Movement before the government came to power, with Blair writing the foreword to a CSM collection of speeches and sermons in 1993.[14] Faith became important to New Labour's Third Way agenda,

---

[11] Interview with Iqbal Sacranie, 8/3/2011.

[12] The Lambeth Group met at Lambeth Palace, was co-chaired by the Archbishop's chaplain and a senior civil servant at the Department for Culture, Media and Sport, and brought together representatives of the five largest faiths and other stakeholders. Its achievements included designing the Faith Zone at the Millennium Dome and providing guidelines for inter-faith acts of reflection. See Home Office Faith Communities Unit (2004) *Working Together: Co-operation between Government and Faith Communities*. London: Faith Communities Unit, Home Office, p. 10.

[13] Liat Radcliffe, "A Muslim Lobby at Whitehall? Examining the Role of the Muslim Minority in British Foreign Policy Making," in *Islam and Christian–Muslim Relations*, Vol. 15, No. 3, 2004, pp. 365-386. These changes in New Labour's recognition of faith were not universally celebrated by faith actors, or even by Muslims. The MCB's status was particularly controversial, and many other Muslim organisations started in the 1990s and 2000s challenged this. See the chapter on "Representation" in our publication *Taking Part*, referenced in endnote 3.

[14] Tony Blair, "Foreword," in Christopher Bryant, ed. (1993) *Reclaiming the Ground: Christianity and Socialism*. London: Spire. For analyses of New Labour's public approach to

influenced in particular by the communitarianism of Amitai Etzioni and the "social capital" perspective of Robert Putnam.[15] Religious congregations were increasingly seen as reservoirs of under-tapped and responsible voluntarism that could be channeled into the government's initiatives for civil renewal. The term "faith," rather than religion, became the more positive and preferred term for a variety of political uses.

Broader changes in public management, expressed in the government white paper *Modern Local Government: In Touch with the People* (1998), facilitated the development of faith sector governance at a local level throughout the country. These changes included increases in funding for urban regeneration (e.g., the New Deal for Communities), extending consumer choices in welfare,[16] and introducing Local Strategic Partnerships (LSPs) in which key stakeholders took part in local co-governance. LSPs were required to "make specific efforts to involve and consult faith communities," with the result that faith representatives became increasingly visible in these local governance bodies.[17] Professor Michael Keith, who served as Leader of the Tower Hamlets Council in the early 2000s, summarises the various changes as the "pluralisation of the sites of the political," meaning a multiplication of the institutional spaces in which political decision-making and activism took place.[18] The work of the ICRC helped to ensure that faith was explicitly included in this programme of modernisation. In 1997 the ICRC contributed to a chapter on "Involving Faith Communities" in the DETR document *Involving Communities in Urban and Rural Regeneration: A Guide for Practitioners*. An Inter Faith Network conference in Birmingham in 2000 led to a document on local authorities' faith engagement called *Faith and*

---

faith see the essays in Elaine L. Graham, ed. (2009) *Doing God? Public Theology under Blair*. London: Continuum.

[15] Robert Putnam devotes a chapter in *Bowling Alone* to the decline of religious participation, and many of his works emphasise that religious congregations are important bearers of social capital (e.g., *Better Together, American Grace*). Amitai Etzioni, when writing about the positive social effects of community bonds, states that "The strongest evidence for these statements is found in religious communities that meet my definition of shared affective bonds and a moral culture." See Amitai Etzioni (2000) *The Third Way to a Good Society*. London: Demos, p. 9.

[16] John Clarke et al., (2007) *Creating Citizen-Consumers: Changing Public and Changing Public Services*. London: Sage.

[17] Adam Dinham and Vivien Lowndes, "Religion, Resources, and Representation: Three Narratives of Faith Engagement in British Urban Governance," in *Urban Affairs Review*, Vol. 43, No. 6, 2008, pp. 817-845.

[18] Interview with Michael Keith, 29/2/2012.

Community (2002), the joint product of the LGA, ICRC, IFN, and Home Office Active Community Unit. The document speaks often of faith groups as "constituencies" and argues for their inclusion in various levels and procedures of local governance.

Official documents such as these show the growing influence of the ICRC and IFN, who were working hard to ensure their voices were heard. In 1998, Hilary Armstrong MP, the Minister for Local Government and Housing, appointed a review team to evaluate the performance of the ICRC. The team, consisting of Bishop John Austin and former Home Office official Roy Taylor, produced a review document that argued the ICRC was having "a considerable impact through the subtle permeation of the culture of Government."[19] The ICRC had built relationships with civil servants and key ministers that seem to have facilitated some of the faith-related advances in New Labour's first term. Yet the review team also voiced a concern that the Council's effectiveness in raising faith issues had not been accompanied by substantial success in its regeneration remit. It noted that this was due, in part, to the interest ICRC members were taking in "faith, identity and citizenship" issues. Jenny Taylor has argued that Muslim members of the ICRC, particularly Iqbal Sacranie, were increasingly setting the agenda in meetings on issues such as discrimination and Islamophobia. In Taylor's view this was a process that "can be legitimately termed 'Islamisation.'"[20]

Whilst the ICRC had evolved into a more general faith consultative body with less of an exclusive focus on regeneration, "Islamisation" is a misnomer since the change had been consistently inter-faith. A good example can be seen in the advocacy for a religion question in the Census. The minutes of an ICRC meeting in January 1996 record that "members of the faith organisations expressed general support for testing a question on religious affiliation, for possible inclusion in the 2001 Census."[21] Based on this internal consensus, the ICRC wrote an initial enquiry to the Office of National Statistics suggesting a religion

[19] Bishop John Austin and Roy Taylor (1998) *Review of the Inner Cities Religious Council.* Review document commissioned by Hilary Armstrong MP.
[20] Jenny Taylor, "The Numbers Game: Immigrant Religious Activism, Government Policies and the Interfaith Challenge," in *Centre for Islamic Studies, London School of Theology: CIS Occasional Paper Series*, Vol. 15, 2012, p. 18.
[21] Jamil Sherif, "A Census chronicle – reflections on the campaign for a religion question in the 2001 Census for England and Wales," in *Journal of Beliefs & Values: Studies in Religion & Education*, Vol. 32, No. 1, 2011, pp. 1-18.

question be considered. The ICRC, MCB, and IFN then worked together over the next four years to build a coalition across faith traditions that advocated the inclusion of a religion question. This coalition included leadership from Rev David Randolph-Horn (ICRC), Brian Pearce (IFN), Iqbal Sacranie (MCB), Professor Rev Leslie Francis (Churches Working Together and University of Wales), Marlena Schmool (Board of Deputies of British Jews), and Indarjit Singh (Network of Sikh Organisations).[22] The successful campaign for a religion question in the Census became a striking example of inter-faith collaboration and influence on government during the first New Labour term.

A multi-faith balancing act: 2001-2010

The following three terms of the New Labour government were witness to new challenges connected to the role of religion in public life. Only three months after the 2001 general election came September 11th and the United Kingdom's subsequent participation in the "War on Terror." And only two months after the 2005 election came the UK's own domestic experience of terrorism in the 7/7 London bombings – all of which served to intensify attention on Muslims and Islam in Britain. The invasions of Afghanistan and Iraq led many British Muslims to protest and lobby the government on foreign policy, emerging disillusioned when their efforts came to no avail.[23] Some have argued that the Prevent strategy of "winning hearts and minds" of British Muslims to prevent violent extremism was counterproductive because it cast Muslims as a "suspect community."[24]   Prevent may have had some positive results as well, but it undeniably frayed trust between British Muslims and the government.[25]

---

[22] Ibid.

[23] Liat Radcliffe, "A Muslim Lobby at Whitehall? Examining the Role of the Muslim Minority in British Foreign Policy Making," in *Islam and Christian–Muslim Relations*, Vol. 15, No. 3, 2004, pp. 365-386.

[24] Christina Pantazis and Simon Pemberton, "From the 'Old' to the 'New' Suspect Community: Examining the Impacts of Recent UK Counter-Terrorist Legislation," in *British Journal of Criminology*, Vol. 49, No. 5, 2009, pp. 646-666.

[25] Paul Thomas, "Failed and Friendless: The UK's 'Preventing Violent Extremism' Programme," in *The British Journal of Politics & International Relations*, Vol. 12, No. 3, 2010, pp. 442-458. We describe some of the positive results of Prevent, particularly in building the capacity of Muslim organizations, in the chapter on "Participation and the Prevent Agenda" of our report *Taking Part: Muslim Participation in Contemporary Governance* (available online at http://bit.ly/takingpart).

The MCB's relationship with New Labour, while close in its first term, faced many ups and downs in the years that followed. The MCB was severely criticised for its decision not to participate in Holocaust Memorial Day.[26] Salma Yaqoob, head of the Birmingham Stop the War Coalition, called this decision of non-participation an "own goal" for the MCB.[27] As the Prevent strategy developed from 2007 onwards, the MCB was also increasingly branded by opponents as an Islamist organisation that was too extreme for government engagement. Its ties with the Department of Communities and Local Government were severed by minister Hazel Blears in March 2009, only to be reinstated by minister John Denham in January 2010, about six months after he took over the department. Finally, the MCB's inability to affect the foreign policy of the Labour government revealed the limits of its influence.[28]

New Labour had invested a great deal of attention in symbolic unity between faiths, particularly in the aftermaths of the 9/11 and 7/7 attacks. A good example of this emphasis on unity can be seen in the Home Office document *Working Together* (2004) which outlined the government's methods for consulting with faith groups. Influenced by the IFN, the document advises that consultations should at a minimum include the five demographically largest faiths in the United Kingdom (Christians, Hindus, Jews, Muslims and Sikhs) and preferably should extend to nine faiths (adding Baha'is, Buddhists, Jains and Zoroastrians). New Labour ministers meticulously balanced the representatives of these faith groups for an appearance of multi-faith consensus.

The government also made an unprecedented level of financial investment in faith groups. Some £13.8 million was spent on the "Faith Communities Capacity Building Fund" from 2006-2008, which was topped up with an additional £7.5 million to accompany the *Face to Face and Side by Side* strategy in 2008. Stephen Timms MP (Labour Party Vice Chairman for Faith Groups) and John Battle MP (the Prime Minister's Faith Envoy) spoke frequently to faith groups to reassure them that

---

[26] The MCB based this decision on the argument that the event should be widened to recognise other victims of atrocities such as contemporary Palestinians.
[27] Salma Yaqoob, "Muslims Need to Take Part," in *The Guardian: Comment is Free*, 21/12/2006, accessed February 2013,
http://www.guardian.co.uk/commentisfree/2006/dec/21/comment.secondworldwar.
[28] Liat Radcliffe, "A Muslim Lobby at Whitehall? Examining the Role of the Muslim Minority in British Foreign Policy Making," in *Islam and Christian–Muslim Relations*, Vol. 15, No. 3, 2004, pp. 365-386.

government was listening and to exhort their civic participation. Various multi-faith or ecumenical networks were founded in the 2000s that established significant relationships with government, most notably the Faith Regen Foundation (2001),[29] the Faith-based Regeneration Network (2002),[30] Faithworks (2002),[31] and FaithAction (2006).[32] The government's *Face to Face and Side by Side* (2008) strategy showed a remarkable religious literacy in terms of its understanding of the ethnic and cultural complexities of religious traditions in Britain and the many roles religion can play in people's lives. The DCLG-commissioned report *Contextualising Islam in Britain* (2009), authored by a team of Muslim scholars and leaders, was even more sophisticated.

Yet the limits of New Labour's multi-faith balancing act were evident from 2006, when the ICRC was replaced by the Faith Communities Consultative Council (FCCC). The FCCC, based at the Home Office and then at the DCLG, was a much larger body than the ICRC had ever been. It incorporated the nine major faiths, and was managed by a civil servant. According to one of our interviewees involved in the FCCC, it "was over-ambitious and it was huge, and in that sense self-defeating."[33] The Coalition government decided to discontinue the FCCC in May 2011, with the then DCLG junior minister Andrew Stunell stating that "we believe that it did not add value to the effective arrangements that

---

[29] The Faith Regen Foundation is a Muslim-inspired multi-faith organisation that focuses on helping ethnic minority and disadvantaged individuals into sustainable employment and on building bridges between faiths. See http://www.faithregenuk.org/AboutUs.html.

[30] The Faith-based Regeneration Network (FbRN) is a multi-faith network that works to facilitate faith-based social action at local level and to improve the policy evidence base. FbRN's Trustees are drawn from each of the nine major faith traditions in the UK. See: http://www.fbrn.org.uk/about-fbrn.

[31] Faithworks began as an ecumenical campaign for greater government recognition of the role of churches and Christian organisations. Led by Baptist minister and social entrepreneur Steve Chalke, the campaign submitted a petition of 70,000 signatures to this effect to 10 Downing Street in the lead up to the 2001 general election. Faithworks then became formalised as an organisation in 2002. It has been well known for its Faithworks Charter of FBO good practice and for its support among prominent politicians including Hazel Blears MP and Prime Minister Tony Blair, who gave a Faithworks lecture in 2005. See http://www.faithworks.info/about-us/what-we-do.

[32] FaithAction is a network of faith-based organisations that provides information, training, and links with government. It was initially established and co-managed by LifeLine, Faithworks, and Faith Regen Foundation as one of the two strategic partners of the government's Office of the Third Sector (the other strategic partner was the Church Urban Fund). FaithAction has since evolved into its own organisation, now in strategic partnership with the Department of Health, and among other roles serves as secretariat to the APPG on Faith and Society. See: http://www.faithaction.net/index.php?p=82.

[33] Interview, undated to protect anonymity.

Departments already have in place for consulting faith communities on policy."[34]

A larger question emerging in the latter years of New Labour concerned whether the government's interest in faith had been little more than a thinly concealed interest in Muslims. The more than £60 million New Labour's Prevent counter-terrorism agenda provided to local authorities, focused on Muslims alone, easily dwarfed its general faith capacity building programmes.[35] This disparity did not go unnoticed by those in other faith traditions, and led some to speak of the PVE (Preventing Violent Extremism) as "Promoting Virulent Envy."[36] Meanwhile the report *Moral, But No Compass* (2008), commissioned by the Anglican Bishop for Urban Life and Faith Stephen Lowe, argued that the New Labour government had provided little more than "lip service" to the importance of the Church of England.[37] The report observed that there was a "perceived discrimination against the Christian Church and other religious bodies" in central government policies and a "relative downgrading of regional and other local actors." The report's authors found that the Conservatives had "at the least, a *rhetorical* desire to address many of these issues" (emphasis original). They expressed optimism that a Conservative government might begin to get the balance right.

---

[34] Hansard, HC Deb, 23 June 2011, c440W.

[35] The Department of Communities and Local Government distributed a total of £61.7 million to local authorities under New Labour's Prevent programme. Prevent funding to the OSCT in the Home Office was substantially larger, and funding was also provided to the Foreign and Commonwealth Office for Prevent work abroad. For a breakdown of Prevent spending see HM Government (2011) *Prevent Strategy*. London: The Stationery Office, pp. 100-102. See also Arun Kundnani (2009) *Spooked: How Not To Prevent Violent Extremism*. London: Institute of Race Relations, pp. 11-12.

[36] Yahya Birt, "Promoting Virulent Envy?: Reconsidering the UK's Terrorism Prevention Strategy," in *The RUSI Journal*, Vol. 154, No. 4, 2009, pp. 52-58.

[37] Francis Davis, Elizabeth Paulhus, and Andrew Bradstock (2008) *Moral, But No Compass: Government, Church and the Future of Welfare*. Chelmsford, UK: Matthew James Publishing. This report received substantial attention, including featuring as the lead story in *The Times* (7 June 2008) and being the subject of a House of Lords debate on 9 October 2008. For more on the report's influence on thinking within the Church of England, see the General Synod note GS Misc 912 by Bishop Stephen Lowe, available online at: http://www.churchofengland.org/media/38972/gsmisc912.pdf.

Faith in the coalition since 2010: "a Christian country"

Following the May 2010 general election, the Conservatives and Liberal Democrats formed a coalition government with David Cameron at its helm. From the beginning this coalition has sought to differentiate itself from New Labour in its approach to faith. In a speech commemorating the 400th anniversary of the King James Bible, David Cameron offered an explicit and confident statement on the role of religion within British public and political life, arguing that although "People often say politicians shouldn't 'do God,'" in fact, politicians should recognise "both what our faith communities bring to our country … and also how incredibly important faith is to many people in Britain."[38] By invoking and overturning Alistair Campbell's phrase "we don't do God," the Prime Minister was attempting to put clear blue water between the coalition and New Labour's position on the role of religion in public life. Indeed, the same "doing God" message has been reiterated since then by government ministers.[39]

Yet, as we have already seen, New Labour actually *did* do God throughout all of its thirteen years in power. It engaged with faith more extensively and self-consciously than any previous modern British government. The coalition's interest in faith, then, should not be understood as a signal of a new era so much as a continuation of this trend.

That being said, David Cameron can justly argue that the content of his government's approach to faith differs from that of New Labour. The critical shift has been from a multi-faith paradigm to a Christian heritage focus. In the same King James Bible speech, Cameron locates Christianity at the centre of British public life: "We are a Christian country. And we should not be afraid to say so."[40] Public statements by Baroness Sayeeda Warsi have invoked the need to emphasise and protect Christian heritage in the face of encroaching secularism. In a speech to the Vatican, Warsi argued that "Europe needs to be more confident in its

---

[38] David Cameron, "Prime Minister's King James Bible Speech," 16/12/2011.
[39] The message that the coalition "does God" has been conveyed by minister Baroness Warsi in multiple statements and has been reiterated by communities minister Eric Pickles: "Alastair Campbell declared 'we don't do God.' By contrast, I think this government does." Eric Pickles, "A Christian Ethos Strengthens Our Nation," in *The Telegraph*, 12/9/2012, accessed February 2013, http://www.telegraph.co.uk/news/religion/9538561/A-Christian-ethos-strengthens-our-nation.html.
[40] Cameron, "King James Bible."

Christianity."[41]   Relatedly, when a high court ruled that Christian prayers in the Bideford Town Council were unlawful, communities minister Eric Pickles intervened by expediting the "general power of competence" for councils in the Localism Act 2011, and argued that this applies to a competence to continue to hold council prayers. Pickles saw this as necessary because "for too long, the public sector has been used to marginalise and attack faith in public life, undermining the very foundations of the British nation."[42] In a major speech in early 2013 he argued that "in recent years long-standing British liberties of freedom of religion have been undermined by the intolerance aggressive secularism."[43]

In all of these statements, key leaders in the coalition seem to be attempting to correct the "perceived discrimination against the Christian Church and other religious bodies" which had been noted in *Moral, But No Compass*. Lobby groups such as Christian Concern and senior figures including Lord George Carey and Lord Michael Nazir-Ali have argued that Christians are facing "persecution" in British public life, particularly due to high profile legal cases.[44] Interestingly, Lord Rowan Williams, while Archbishop of Canterbury, expressed his dissatisfaction with the persecution argument.[45]   But at least in certain wings of the Church of England and of the Conservative Party, the government's recognition of Britain's Christian heritage as valuable yet under threat has been welcomed. Unfortunately for the government, the same constituencies who support its bold words on Christianity overlap considerably with those who feel alienated by its bill to introduce same-sex marriage.

In terms of policy, the coalition has to a large degree brought engagement with the faith sector under the banner of Big Society. In this respect, the coalition's emphasis on Christian heritage has been accompanied by a renewal of inter-faith work. Speaking at the AGM of the Inter Faith Network, the then DCLG minister Andrew Stunell

---

[41] Baroness Sayeeda Warsi, "Militant Secularism Speech," 13/2/2012.
[42] BBC News, "Councils Win Prayer 'Rights' as Localism Act Powers Fast Tracked, Ministers Say," 18/2/2012, accessed February 2013, http://www.bbc.co.uk/news/uk-politics-17082136.
[43] Eric Pickles, "Uniting our communities: integration in 2013," speech delivered to Policy Exchange and British Future event, 15/1/2013, accessed February 2013, https://www.gov.uk/government/speeches/uniting-our-communities-integration-in-2013.
[44] See Michael Nazir-Ali (2012) *Triple Jeopardy for the West: Aggressive Secularism, Radical Islamism and Multiculturalism*. London: Bloomsbury Continuum.
[45] Rowan Williams (2012) *Faith in the Public Square*. London: Bloomsbury Continuum.

explained that "Inter faith activity is more important than ever in our work towards the Big Society, so I want to push for more inter-faith dialogue and action rather than individual faith groups delivering social projects."[46] Near Neighbours, a new programme funded by the DCLG, brings together the inter-faith and Christian heritage aspects of the Coalition's engagement with religion in a very interesting way, and is worthy of exploring in some detail.

Near Neighbours

Near Neighbours is a coalition initiative providing £5 million funding to promote interactions across faith and non-faith groups. The programme was launched in Autumn 2011 in four urban centres across England: Birmingham, Bradford, Leicester, and part of East London.[47] About £3 million of the funds are designated for a set of larger bodies including the Christian Muslim Forum, the Council of Christians and Jews, the Hindu Christian Forum, and the Feast, all of which do extensive work across faiths.[48] The Near Neighbours Fund portion, at £2 million, is devoted to small pots of money of between £250 and £5,000 given to local groups for projects that bring people of different backgrounds together through a simple application process. In many ways this Big Society initiative seems designed to give greater autonomy to faith groups and let local communities generate their own solutions. What is novel is that the programme is being administered by the Church Urban Fund, which allocates the funding, and applicants require the counter-signature of the vicar from the parish in which the proposed project will take place.

There has been unease among some, including Church of England clergy, about the Church being placed in this role. To others, the reach and richness of the Church of England's infrastructure, as well as its history of inter-faith work, are valuable resources to make this programme work.

---

[46] Andrew Stunell is a Liberal Democrat MP. During David Cameron's reshuffle, he stepped down from his ministerial role at the Department of Communities and Local Government.
[47] For more information on Near Neighbours and the specific areas in which it is operating, see the programme website: http://www.cuf.org.uk/near-neighbours.
[48] Interview with Guy Wilkinson, 9/2/2012.

Muslim civil society reactions to Near Neighbours have ranged from critical to positive.[49] One critic of the programme is Abdul-Rehman Malik, a public intellectual and journalist based in Tower Hamlets. Malik is deeply concerned about the Near Neighbours structure: "Do you think Muslims know which parish they're part of?" he asked, incredulously, "To me, it's undemocratic."[50] Ataullah Siddiqui of the Markfield Institute in Leicester noted that "this government's funding policy has just the opposite of what the previous government's was [because] they want to channel money through the Church of England." He added, "now, I'm not sure if it is a good thing or a bad thing," but it raises several questions because "until recently the Church was, as far as the money from government is concerned, one of the many faith communities. Now it has seized the moment – they are the one now with the control and the power. So how do you relate to that? And what will the impact be?"[51]

Some other Muslim governance and civil society actors speak of Near Neighbours and the Church's role in it in much more positive terms. Maqsood Ahmed, who was involved in the DCLG development of the programme, believes that Near Neighbours provides a structure by which to support the development of other faith groups, including Muslims: "[The] Church of England is well established, they have a wonderful infrastructure. Why don't we use them as a kind of ground to get others involved?"[52] Ibrahim Mogra, an imam in Leicester who is nationally prominent, likewise spoke of the Church's infrastructure as a major strength. He said it is a refreshing change from Prevent and could "achieve the results that the Prevent agenda wanted to achieve, but it's more palatable." Mogra placed his advocacy for the programme in the context of broader issues of faith in British public life: "I would want to make sure that the Church remains strong in this country because in that lies our safety. We can turn to them and they can take us under their safety net, if you like. If the Church of England falls, God help us, what's going to happen to the Muslims and Hindus and everybody else?"[53]

---

[49] For a somewhat more detailed version of this analysis of Near Neighbours, including the views of a broader range of Muslim and government actors, see the chapter on "The Faith Sector" in our report *Taking Part: Muslim Participation in Contemporary Governance* (available online at http://bit.ly/takingpart).

[50] Interview with Abdul-Rehman Malik, 30/11/2011.

[51] Interview with Ataullah Siddiqui, 23/11/2011.

[52] Interview with Maqsood Ahmed, 3/4/2012.

[53] Interview with Ibrahim Mogra, 16/1/2012.

It is clear that from the government's perspective, the Church of England's central role in Near Neighbours is seen as a strength. Eric Pickles, the DCLG minister responsible for the Near Neighbours funding, describes it in this way: "Christians also have the right to be heard by policy-makers. In my own government department, we have funded the Near Neighbours programme, working with the Church Urban Fund and its parish network to build stronger communities."[54] With the idea that Christians "have the right to be heard," Pickles is connecting Near Neighbours into the narrative that the Christian heritage of Britain should be bolstered and defended.

From studying how Near Neighbours is implemented on the ground, further nuances emerge. We have conducted in-depth research in three of the four Near Neighbours areas: Birmingham, Leicester, and Tower Hamlets. The local Near Neighbours programme coordinators in these areas and the central operational staff at the Church Urban Fund have all been meticulously careful to ensure that funding goes to a diverse set of faith, inter-faith, and non-faith groups, with a diversity of project participants. The Church of England's reputation with the programme, of course, stands or falls on the basis that it does not show favouritism.

In terms of the lead-organisations that receive Near Neighbours funds, Christian organisations (83) do outnumber Muslim organisations (21), at a rate of 4 to 1.[55] This is unsurprising, given that the programme is administered at parish-level and clergy are kept well informed about it. However in the average first-year Near Neighbours project, 39% of participants have been Muslim. This was the largest proportion of any single faith group, greater than the 36% who were Christian. It seems that while the parish system may favour Christian groups as recipients of funding, the beneficiaries of Near Neighbours services and activities have to the largest extent been Muslims.[56] The high level of Muslim

---

54 Pickles. "A Christian Ethos."

55 These figures, and all numbers included in this paragraph, are from the short document prepared by Stephen Tunstall of the Church Urban Fund for our research project, Stephen Tunstall, "Near Neighbours and Muslim Participation," Church Urban Fund memo, 5 October 2012.

56 It is important to note that the largest number of lead-organisations in the first year of Near Neighbours have been classified as "non-faith based" community groups. These accounted for the leadership of 156 projects, or over half of the 307 in total. It is also the case that some lead-organisations that might have been described as "Muslim" have preferred to be included in a "non-faith based" category (e.g., identifying as a Somali organisations). The figure of 21 Muslim-led projects, then, understates the number of

participation in Near Neighbours projects reflects at least three dynamics – the selection of the four Near Neighbours Fund locations in areas of high Muslim concentration;[57] an interest among Christian clergy and inter-faith leaders in involving Muslims; and high levels of Muslim engagement that carry over from the investment by the previous government. Indeed, perhaps the most interesting aspect of Near Neighbours participation is that the typical project involves Muslims and Christians, but not necessarily people from other faiths. A total of only 7 projects in the programme's first year were led by organisations from "other faiths," which amounts to only a third of the number led by Muslim organisations alone. New Labour's large-scale investment in Muslims, followed by the Coalition's investment Christianity, has perhaps helped facilitate a "bipolar" environment of faith relations. This is not necessarily a criticism, but a reflection that central government's faith sector funding now follows the precedent of the Church of England's Christian Muslim Forum more than any other model.[58]

Conclusion

This chapter has traced some of the key national-level developments in the emergence of a "faith paradigm" in public policy, including the importance of inter-faith work and the role of faith in policy documents and consultative bodies, particularly in relation to Muslims. We have shown the importance of Faith in the City and the Rushdie Affair in catalysing religious actors' engagement with the state, which became institutionalised in the Inner Cities Religious Council, Inter Faith Network, and Muslim Council of Britain. New Labour's engagement with faith through these bodies and otherwise was very extensive, even if problematic, particularly in its provision of funds through faith capacity building and the Prevent Strategy.

---

projects that could be placed in this category (as do the figures for Christian-led and other faith-led projects, for similar reasons).

[57] Near Neighbours builds upon the Church of England's Presence & Engagement (P&E) programme. The Near Neighbours areas programme managers are based in four pre-existing P&E centres. A major goal of the P&E programme has been to maintain the relevance of the Church of England in areas where church attendance may be low and other religious groups, quite often Muslims, have grown numerically.

[58] Indeed, the Christian Muslim Forum is a Presence & Engagement group that has been funded by Near Neighbours.

The Conservative-led coalition government has shown a rhetorical interest in faith that is at least the equal of New Labour's. However the Christian-specificity of ministerial statements on faith, and particularly David Cameron's phrase "we are a Christian country," may be narrowing the ability of the government to speak to the demographically diversifying population of multi-faith Britain. A key challenge for the government is to more clearly articulate what a "Christian country" is understood to mean and how it can accommodate the various strands of religious life in Britain. Professor Paul Weller has described the religious landscape in Britain today as "three dimensional," by which he means simultaneously Christian, secular, and religiously plural.[59] In holding this balance together, Baroness Sayeeda Warsi, the first Muslim to serve in a British Cabinet, can be a real asset to the Coalition and it would be unfortunate for government to be hesitant in deploying this "secret weapon."[60] Indeed, Muslims are not outliers but allies with other faith actors in supporting a religious presence in governance and public life. If the Christian heritage of Britain can be successfully pluralised to incorporate minority faiths in a meaningful way, the government will find many willing allies for continuing establishment as a way of ensuring the presence of faith in public life.

---

[59] Paul Weller (2005) *Time for a Change: Reconfiguring Religion, State and Society*. London: T&T Clark.

[60] Mehdi Hasan. "Not a Dull Grey Man in a Suit," in *The New Statesman*, 3 April 2012, accessed February 2013, http://www.newstatesman.com/politics/2012/04/sayeeda-warsi-asian-voters. While Sadiq Khan MP became the first Muslim to attend cabinet, as a minister for transport, he was not a member of the cabinet. Sayeeda Warsi served as Co-Chair of the Conservative Party from May 2010-September 2012 and member of David Cameron's cabinet.

Attending to the Spirit in Mental Health
Peter Gilbert

I have now got a psychiatrist who is a Christian, which is helpful, as sometimes I have been sectioned (under the 1983 Mental Health Act) because of the confusion by psychiatrists between genuine belief and religious mania. Service user in conversation with the author, 2012

Introduction

There is perhaps a popular perception of a current standoff between religion and science, but the reality is much more complex than that because all human strivings for meaning, and our beliefs and belief systems, are designed to make sense of our world and the universe at large. Within science there are intense disputes between various models of evolutionary theory, and biologists often clash with physicists and cosmologists. Physicist and cosmologist Paul Davies, in his masterly overview of our universe and how it works, states that:

> Like the porridge in the tale of Goldilocks and the three bears, the universe seems to be "just right" for life, in many intriguing ways. No scientific explanation for the universe can be deemed complete unless it accounts for this appearance of judicious design.[1]

Rather than getting into a conceptual disputation, Chief Rabbi, Dr Jonathan Sacks, in his latest book, talks about a partnership between faith and science, and points out that human beings are "meaning-seeking animals. It is what makes us unique. To be human is to ask the question 'why?'"[2]

---

[1] Paul Davies (2006) *The Goldilocks Enigma: Why is the Universe Just Right for Life?* London: Allen Lane, p. 3.

[2] Jonathan Sacks (2011) *The Great Partnership: God, Science and the Search for Meaning.* London: Hodder and Stoughton.

It is noteworthy that many films in recent years have been centred around the mystery of life. Whether these are about extra-terrestrials, vampires or angels, cinema, which has to appeal to the public's interests, has been considering the mystical and immaterial. Professor Brian Cox's superb BBC2 series, *Wonders of the Universe* (2012), is an example of Professor Richard Dawkins' perhaps belated suggestion that the "magic" needs to be brought back into science. Professor Cox is an atheist, but he starts off each episode asking the continuing human questions: "Where do we come from? Why are we here?" One might also ask, as many people do when they reach a health crisis, "Where do we go to when we die?"

In the field of health the splendid advances in medical science have sometimes too much of a "left brain hemisphere" (hyper-rational) approach, leaving out the more meaning-making and emotional aspects of the right hemisphere of the brain. In mental health, service users and their carers have increasingly requested services' attention to their spiritual strengths and needs,[3] and the work by Harold Koenig and colleagues in the USA,[4] as well as neuropsychiatrists like Peter Fenwick in the UK,[5] has demonstrated the vital importance of an individual's inner spirit (psyche), their sense of the transcendent (pneuma) and their beliefs and belief systems, including faith communities, in maintaining health and recovery from physical and/or mental illnesses.

As the quotation from the service user at the beginning of this chapter demonstrates, it is sometimes difficult to have one's beliefs taken seriously. But human beings are all about seeking meaning, and as the playwright Tom Stoppard put it: "When we have found all the mysteries and lost all the meaning, we will be alone, on an empty shore."[6]

---

[3] Peter Gilbert, ed. (2011) *Spirituality and Mental Health*. Brighton: Pavilion.
[4] Harold G. Koenig, Dana E. King, and Verna Benner Carson (2012) *Handbook of Religion and Health*. Oxford: Oxford University Press.
[5] Peter Fenwick, "Neuroscience of the spirit," in Chris Cook, Andrew Powell and Andrew Sims, eds. (2009) *Spirituality and Psychiatry*. London: RCPsych.
[6] Tom Stoppard (1993) *Arcadia*. London: Faber and Faber, Act 2, Scene 7.

A phoenix from the flames

If you want to make God laugh tell him what you have planned for tomorrow! Father
Michael Judge, the chaplain to the New York Fire Service who died rescuing
people after the 9/11 attacks in New York

In the autumn of 2001 Professor Antony Sheehan was setting up the
National Institute for Mental Health in England (NIMHE), an
organisation which connected developing government policy on mental
health with research and practice both regionally and locally. England
has an unfortunate tradition of not always connecting the centre with the
regions and the front line of practice; NIMHE was an excellent example
of just how to do this and increase learning and the spread of good
practice at all levels.[7] I joined NIMHE as the representative to take
forward issues around Social Work and Social Care in mental health.[8] At
the first meeting I attended in September 2011, two weeks after the tragic
Al-Qaeda attacks on New York, something impelled me to ask whether
9/11 might have a specifically detrimental effect on the mental health of
many Muslims, and indeed whether it might shape the world view of
many in the general population. We now know from the research by
Koenig et al. that following the 9/11 attacks "Americans flooded into
churches, prayed and bought Bibles like they were going out of print,"
though, as time passed, religious coping returned to pre-trauma levels.[9]
NIMHE was already undertaking work around the needs of people from
ethnic minorities, but Professor Sheehan, as a leader with a vision,
decided that it was important to consider individuals' spiritual needs
and build networks with faith communities. He asked me to follow these
ideas up and scope the issues.

A few weeks later I was on a panel at a conference in the East Midlands,
and introduced myself as the NIMHE spokesperson on social care and
social work, adding, in a quiet voice, that I also had responsibility for
spirituality. Much to my surprise, the large audience almost
unanimously said that that's what they wanted to talk about because if
they mentioned spirituality or God to their consultant psychiatrist then

---

[7] Peter Gilbert and Michael Clark, "Waking the sleeping giant: reflections on leadership and
the National Institute for Mental Health in England (NIMHE) 2002-2009," in *The
International Journal of Leadership in Public Services*, Vol. 6, No. 2, June 2010.
[8] Peter Gilbert et al. (2010) *Social Work and Mental Health: The Value of Everything*. Lyme
Regis: Russell House Publishing.
[9] Koenig, King and Carson, *Handbook*, p. 96.

the medication was increased! (It is important to state that the Royal College of Psychiatrists set up a special interest group on Spirituality and Mental Health in 1999 which, with Professor Chris Cook as its current Chair, has produced very helpful guidance, see: www.rcpsych.ac.uk/spirit.)

My acknowledgement of the strength of feeling at this conference, and then my scoping of the issue across a range of faith-based and professional organisations and universities, led to NIMHE setting up a specific Project on Spirituality and Mental Health (see Box 1).

Box 1: The National Spirituality and Mental Health Project

The objectives of the project are to:

i.   Chart what is known and who is doing what in terms of:
- The role of spirituality in mental health
- The role of religion in mental health
- The role of faith communities in mental health
- The relationship between MH services and belief communities

ii.   Identify areas of good practice across mental health as a whole.

iii.   Build coalitions of individuals and groups, and establish links internationally.

iv.   Originally to set up "pilot sites"/collaboratives linked to regional development centres/regional health bodies, which would learn from, test, develop and promote positive practice, and support regional networks. (The Forum has been working to establish positive links with all 60+ Mental Health Trusts in England.)

v.   Develop and create linkages with the other Department of Health initiatives and other relevant governmental programmes.

vi.   Bring together the growing body of research evidence on the importance of spirituality in mental health, and stimulate further research.

vii.   Influence curriculum formation for all professional groups and strengthen staff development at a front-line level.

viii.   Support the role of chaplains (from all appropriate belief systems) as part of the multi-disciplinary team.

ix.   Assist in the production of national, regional and local policy guidance, linked with the CPA and other assessment and care planning processes, and influence training programmes.

x.	Promote specific projects which will enable faith communities to better include and support those coping with the effects of mental distress and mental ill-health in their community.
xi.	Broaden the understanding of clinical outcomes so as to include service user goals.
xii.	Encourage staff to recognise their needs as "whole-persons," and work with organisations to support this.
xiii.	Work with appropriate bodies e.g. journalists and training organisations to promote and develop good practice.

I was fortunate to be able to draw upon Professor John Swinton's seminal book on spirituality as "a forgotten dimension" in mental health to help me set out with service users across the country the direction in which we should go.[10]

A Pilgrimage of Empathic Ignorance

It is now time to put the psyche back into psychological therapy and open the doors and windows of our souls. Salma Khalid, 2011

In a recent publication of the narratives of mental health survivors, *Voices of Experiences*, many of those telling their story mention the importance of their belief system.[11] Psychologist Peter Chadwick, for example, tells us that his "journey was one of 'total psychology' – from cognitive neurochemistry to the socio-political and spiritual. Therefore, my recovery was a product of science, heart and spirituality."[12]

My own journey, described in the same publication, also embraces a number of facts on the road to recovery.[13] Experiencing a major work-related depression I was very fortunate to have an understanding,

---

[10] John Swinton (2001) *Spirituality and Mental Health: Rediscovering a 'Forgotten' Dimension.* London: Jessica Kingsley Publishers.

[11] Thurstine Basset and Theo Stickley, eds. (2010) *Voices of Experience: Narratives of Mental Health Survivors.* Chichester: Wiley-Blackwell.

[12] Peter Chadwick, "The antidote to madness: crystallising out the real self," in Basset and Stickley, *Narratives*, pp. 13-19.

[13] Peter Gilbert, "The bridge of sighs and the bridge of love," in Bassett and Stickley, *Narratives*, pp. 95-113.

humane and expert GP who prescribed the right medication for me but was also careful to take into account the other sources of support available. One of these was a Benedictine Monastery (Worth Abbey) with whom I have had a long standing relationship, and who welcomed me back for a period of spiritual succour. For me, depression can be summed up in one word: "disconnection." I felt disconnected, or unplugged, from people, nature and God. When sitting with the monks in the choir stall at the set times of office (prayer), I didn't have to actively participate. Just listening to and absorbing the prayers of the monks who had befriended me buoyed me up and lifted my spirits. Abbot Stephen also spent a great deal of time listening to the issues which were afflicting me, for which I owe him a great debt of gratitude. Another resource was my running club, Black Pear Joggers of Worcester.[14] Running not only helped me connect with myself and with nature, it also boosted my endorphins, providing a natural anti-depressant to assist the medication. Knowing that a group of friends would be running at the same time every week helped me to get out of my chair in front of day time television (!) and go and exercise. Although the depression meant that I often didn't feel like directly communicating with people, running in a group meant that I could experience a sense of community, camaraderie and communion without necessarily communicating.

It is important to stress the complementarity of what Peter Chadwick calls "total psychology," combining medicine, psychological approaches, relationships, the inner spirit and motivating force, the sense of connectedness to others and the other, and our personal creativity, as appropriate. A social work colleague tells of working with an Afro-Caribbean woman who was a Pentecostal Christian, and suffered post natal depression. Initially, the woman was not keen to take medication, as she saw this as a lack of faith in God's healing power. However, the social worker, through her sensitive work with the individual, her family, her Pentecostal pastor and the mental health trust chaplaincy team, managed to avoid intervention through the Mental Health Act, and the individual began to take the medication as well as gaining great support and solace from her faith and religious community.[15]

---

[14] See Peter Gilbert, "Keep up your spirits," *Open Mind*, Issue 135, September/October 2005.
[15] Gilbert et al., *Social Work*, pp. 114-115.

Recently a leaflet has been produced for Muslims, again urging the importance of combining a faith with contact with statutory services.[16]

Box 2: Spirituality Conferences

1. NIMHE/Mental Health Foundation/Pavilion Conferences:
    *   *Breath of Life: Spirituality and Mental Health*, 2003
    *   *Drinking from the Wells of our Humanity*, 2004

2. NIMHE/National Spirituality and Mental Health Forum:
    *   Conference for spirituality and pastoral care leads and other staff from mental health trusts, 2006

3. NIMHE/Staffordshire University/National Forum:
    *   *Nurturing Heart and Spirit: Belief Systems and Mental Health*, 2006[17]
    *   *From the Cradle – to Beyond the Grave? Belief Systems and End of Life Care*, 2008[18]

4. Forum/Staffordshire University:
    *   *The Flourishing City: The Role of Spirituality in Urban Regeneration,* 2009

5. The National Spirituality and Mental Health Forum:
    *   *Colloquium on Dementia Care*, 2010
    *   *National Conference on Spirituality and Mental Health*, 2011

6. Conferences/keynotes also given in Scotland, Wales, Jersey and Guernsey.

We all share the same soul

The National Spirituality and Mental Health Project commenced tentatively in 2001, and gathered momentum as it became clear how important spirituality was to so many people of all faiths and no specific

---

[16] "Feeling Stressed? A Leaflet for Muslims," 4 Minds Project/The Muslim Council of Britain/RCPsych, accessed February 2013, http://www.rcpsych.ac.uk/expertadvice/problems/leafletformuslimsonstress.aspx.

[17] See Peter Gilbert and Halina Kalaga, eds. (2007) *Nurturing Heart and Spirit: Papers from the Multi-Faith Symposium held at Staffordshire University*. Stafford: Staffordshire University/CSIP /The National Spirituality and Mental Health Forum.

[18] Peter Gilbert, "From the Cradle – To Beyond the Grave," *Quality in Ageing and Older Adults*, Vol. 13, No. 3, 2011.

religious faith. From 2003 to 2006, the NIMHE Project was in partnership with the Mental Health Foundation (a national charity), and also worked most closely with the National Spirituality and Mental Health Forum (also now a registered charity: www.mhspirituality.org.uk).[19]

A number of conferences were arranged in partnership (see Box 2), and the foundation for these was the National Project's main focus on:

- Spirituality as an expression of an individual's sense of humanity, and the well springs of how they live their lives and deal with the crises which affect us all. It is, therefore, an essential element in assessment, support and recovery for service users and carers in a whole-person and whole-system approach. It is also vital in the approach to staff, in order to create genuine person-centred organisations.

- The establishment of positive relations with the major religions and belief systems, at a time when an harmonious construct between statutory agencies and faith communities is essential, and when research studies are indicating the benefits of physical and mental health and longevity for those who are members of inclusive and supporting faith communities.[20]

Mind, Body, Heart and Spirit

As you ought not to cure the eyes without the head, or head without the body; so neither ought you to attempt to cure the body without the soul, because the part can never be well unless the whole be well. Plato

As Peter Chadwick puts it, we are sometimes too dominated by the "impersonal fact-finding empiricism that currently dominates our subject".[21] The experience of individuals and communities, and the research[22] continually emphasises the need for a "whole persons and whole systems" approach.[23]

---

[19] Martin Aaron, "Spirituality, the heart of caring," *A life in the day*, Vol. 12, No. 4, November 2008.
[20] Madeleine Parkes with Peter Gilbert (2011) *Report on the Place of Spirituality in Mental Health.* London: National Spirituality and Mental Forum.
[21] Chadwick, "The Antidote," p. 18.
[22] See Parkes with Gilbert, *Report,* and Koenig, King and Carson, *Handbook.*
[23] Gilbert, *Spirituality.*

There is a tendency for some faith communities to be suspicious of statutory services, worrying that they will denigrate people's beliefs and practice. There is also a tendency for statutory services to be suspicious of people's belief systems. One also sometimes hears people say: "Spirituality, ah, you mean religion, and I have problems with religion." In fact, if one goes back to the ancient Greeks, from whom we derive so much of our wisdom, they make it clear that one has to take a whole-person approach, and to quote Plato again: "the part can never be well unless the whole is well."[24]

The features of spirituality concern our meaning and purpose in life: our value base; connecting with others, with the environment and with a sense of the other (God/higher power/the cosmos); and the sense of a journey of self with others. It might be said that a true spirituality cannot be present without a sense of the transcendent and a connection with others and the Other (there cannot be a purely "me" approach, which is too individualistic and consumerist).

Religion encompasses most if not all of the aspects described in definitions of spirituality. These usually occur in the context of belief in, and possibly a personal relationship with, a transcendent being or beings, and adherence to a meta-narrative which seeks to explain the origins of the world and those living in it, as well as the questions which face human beings around life, suffering, death and re-awakening in this world or another.

The great advantage of religious belief in health, as the research indicated, is that it provides a framework for life and a sense of community, and also mutual obligation and altruism. Religion creates a framework within which people seek to understand, interpret and make sense of themselves, their lives and daily experiences, and the universe.

Of course there can be health disadvantages in religion, in that "the framework" can become a "straightjacket." Some religious belief is overly paternalistic, repressive and homophobic, and sometimes loyalty

---

[24] Plato, *Phaedo*, quoted in Linda Ross (1997) *Nurses' Perceptions of Spiritual Care*. Aldershot: Avebury.

to the organisation overtakes the welfare of those for whom it is intended to benefit.[25]

The Project, which moved from NIMHE to the Forum in 2008, has worked with faith communities both through the Forum and through the spiritual and pastoral care department of mental health trusts. From 2008 to 2010 Dr Neil Deuchar, then Medical Director of Birmingham and Solihull Mental Health Foundation Trust, set up a specific research programme on spirituality within the Trust.[26]

Connections were made between NIMHE and then the Forum with all major professional groups and with a number of universities, which had specialist centres for the study of spirituality. These centres led to the formation of the British Association for the Study of Spirituality in 2009 (BASS: www.bassspirituality.org.uk) and has resulted in international conferences held in 2010 and 2012.

Professional groups such as psychiatrists,[27] nursing[28] and social work[29] have demonstrated the value of spirituality in health professions. There is also a strong link with the work of Professor K. W. M. Fulford and values-based practice, which again is gaining ground as those people who use the services and the professionals find a mechanistic tick-box approach increasingly inappropriate.[30]

Box 3: National Guidance from the Project

- Inspiring Hope: recognising the importance of spirituality in a whole person approach to mental health – Gilbert, P. and Nichols, V., NIMHE/MHF, 2003.

- Guidelines on spirituality for staff in acute care services – Gilbert, P., 2008, NIMHE/CSIP/Staffordshire University.

---

[25] See John Swinton (2001) *Spirituality and Mental Health: Rediscovering a "Forgotten" Dimension*. London: Jessica Kingsley Publishers; Parkes with Gilbert, *Report*; Gilbert, *Spirituality*; and Koenig, King and Carson, *Handbook*.

[26] Parkes with Gilbert, *Report*.

[27] See Cook, Powell and Sims, *Psychiatry*.

[28] Wilfred McSherry (2006) *Making Sense of Spirituality in Nursing and Healthcare Practice: An Interactive Approach*. London: Jessica Kingsley Publishers.

[29] Margaret Holloway and Bernard Moss (2011) *Social Work and Spirituality*, Basingstoke, Palgrave MacMillan.

[30] Bill Fulford, Ed Peile and Heidi Carroll (2012) *Essential Values-Based Practice: Clinical Stories Linking Science with People*, Cambridge: Cambridge University Press.

- Report on Spirituality and Mental Health – Parkes with Gilbert, NSMHF, 2011.

- Input to Department of Health, NMHDU, public health, Ministry of Justice and Welsh Government policy document.

Work with faith communities has been of prime importance.[31] Because the Forum has only had four main officers, working one day a week each, a comprehensive approach has clearly been difficult to achieve, but major strides have been made, especially considering the limited resources involved. It has been important to use all opportunities and invitations. For example, when the Project Lead was working also for Birmingham and Solihull Mental Health Trust, he joined the then Head of Spiritual and Pastoral Care (Sandra Thomas) and a psychiatrist (Dr Vinod Singh) in working closely with the Soho Road Gurudwara in Birmingham to talk through the importance of mental health and having an inclusive, non- stigmatising dialogue.

The Project Lead was invited, via a connection through Staffordshire University, to the Karimia Mosque and Institute, Nottingham, to join the community for prayers and then listen to a seminar on mental health, during which there was a very lively and helpful discussion. The Project Lead also spoke at a conference arranged by the Muslim Doctors and Dentists Association.

One-off events are helpful, and these can then be brought into the national seminars arranged by the Forum in London.[32] In September 2012 the Sikh communities and Sikh Health organised a most stimulating and helpful national conference to address these issues.

In 2005 the Church of England (through the work of the Reverend Peter Sedgwick, the late Reverend Christopher Jones and the Venerable Arthur Hawes), in partnership with the Mentality charity and the then NIMHE Project, produced guidelines on mental health for parishes and deaneries in the Church of England. In 2011 the Roman Catholic Church in England and Wales produced their parish pack on mental health:

---

[31] Arthur Hawes and Qaisra Khan, "Faith perspectives on mental health, and work with faith communities," in Gilbert, *Spirituality*, and Gilbert and Kalaga, *Nurturing Heart and Spirit*.

[32] See www.nhspirituality.org.uk.

Welcome me as I am (see www.welcomemeasiam.org.uk) written by Ben Bano (with input from Peter Bates and Peter Gilbert). The Sikh communities are looking to provide a similar resource in 2013, and such a pack could be produced for any of the faith communities, with support from the Forum Project. It is interesting that the Roman Catholic Church in England and Wales have appointed a Bishop (Bishop Richard Moth) to be the National Lead Bishop on mental health – perhaps this is a clue for Government to have a minister for mental health?

With general practitioners and psychiatrists reporting the rates of anxiety and depression are rising – not surprisingly, in the current global financial crisis – faith communities are a resource in physical and mental health, which statutory services need to recognise. Recently, the Chief Rabbi, Dr Jonathan Sacks, has argued: "Religion creates community, community creates altruism and altruism turns us away from self and towards the common good."[33] Interestingly, the late writer Ayn Rand, praised by the 2012 Republican US Vice Presidential candidate, argued in her *The Virtue of Selfishness* that altruism is a "moral corruption," suggesting instead that each person should look out for their own interests.[34] I beg to differ!

Building Trust

…to invalidate a person's spirituality, no matter how distorted that is, is to invalidate that real core sense of self, and I think once you do that you risk doing untold damage to somebody. Service user, the Somerset Spirituality Project[35]

At the October 2011 conference at the Mersey Care Mental Health Trust, with the excellent support from Chair and Chief Executive for Spiritual Care, staff in all professions and at all levels were keen to recognise and attend to service users and carers' spiritual strengths and needs. One of the main questions was how should they do this without transgressing professional boundaries.

NHS Trusts' support for spiritual care/chaplaincy across the UK is patchy. Some Trusts have only a part time chaplain trying desperately to hold things together. Such situations are not helped by the National

---

[33] Gilbert, "From the Cradle."
[34] Ayn Rand (1964/1992) *The Virtue of Selfishness*. New York: Signet.
[35] Quoted in Gilbert, "Cradle," p. 4.

Secular Society's assertion that such care should simply be provided by local faith communities. This very naïve approach completely ignores the complexity of a multicultural, multi-belief society. Some Trusts, however, have appointed proven leaders in the field[36] and have created spiritual care strategies; trained and supported staff; and built relations with a wide range of religious and spiritual communities in their locality. Where this is working well front line staff see their duty as providing a first port of call for an individual's spiritual strengths and needs, with the spiritual and pastoral team acting as a specialist, consultancy resource (see *Diagram 1*).

Increasingly, senior spiritual care leads are undertaking and publishing research in this area,[37] though the UK lags badly behind the USA in this respect.

This approach has been helped by the formation in 2010 of the British Association for the Study of Spirituality, with two highly successful international conferences in 2010 and 2012.

The Forum[38] found that Spiritual Care leads highly valued support and input from a national organisation, since it gave them: an outside, national source of information; connection to other people so as to share good practice; seminars to explore complex issues; input to strategies; and moral support. Looking to the future, a stress was made on the lead for evidence-based practice.[39]

---

[36] See Special Edition of *Mental Health, Religion and Culture*, Vol. 13, No. 6, September 2010.
[37] See Julian Raffay, "Are our mental health practices beyond hope?" *Journal of Healthcare Chaplaincy*, 2012 forthcoming.
[38] Mary Ellen Coyte, "Promoting spirituality in mental health," *Open Mind*, Issue 169, November/December 2011.
[39] Mary Ellen Coyte and Vicky Nichols (2010) *Evaluation Report on Work with Mental Health Trusts*. London: National Spirituality and Mental Health Forum.

Diagram 1

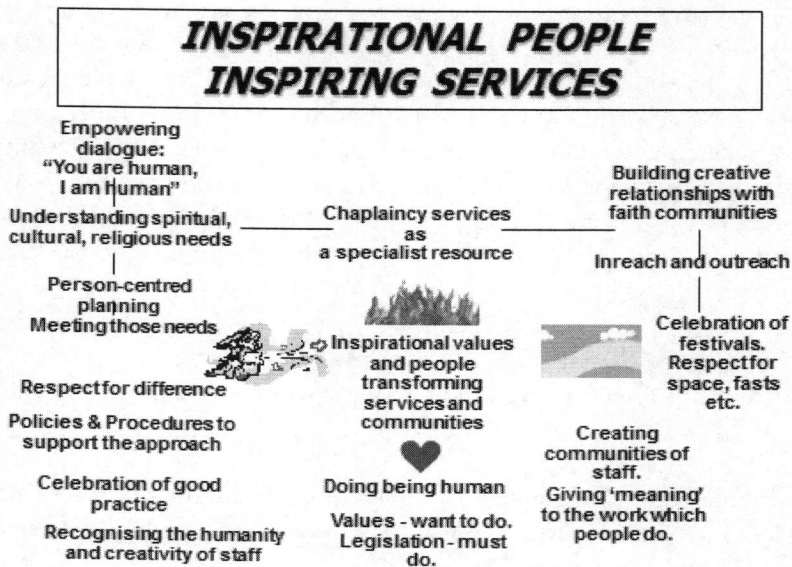

INSPIRATIONAL PEOPLE INSPIRING SERVICES

Empowering dialogue: "You are human, I am human"

Understanding spiritual, cultural, religious needs

Person-centred planning
Meeting those needs

Respect for difference

Policies & Procedures to support the approach

Celebration of good practice

Recognising the humanity and creativity of staff

Chaplaincy services as a specialist resource

Inspirational values and people transforming services and communities

Doing being human

Values - want to do.
Legislation - must do.

Building creative relationships with faith communities

Inreach and outreach

Celebration of festivals. Respect for space, fasts etc.

Creating communities of staff.

Giving 'meaning' to the work which people do.

By kind permission of Jessica Kingsley Publishers.

Conclusion

...as we meet on the path of life. there is one medicine constantly at our disposal that even comes free. This is the power of love, lending hope, giving comfort and helping bring peace to the troubled mind. Andrew Powell

One of the ironies of multiculturalism in the UK is that we were multicultural well before the substantial wave of immigration from the 1950s onwards. As anthropologists point out, there is no such thing as "aboriginal Englishmen" because the last ice age saw human beings leave the UK and move towards the Ukraine, and northern Spain amongst other venues. Over the centuries waves of immigration and invasion have occurred, and although we speak of England as an "Anglo-Saxon nation," genetically it is nothing of the sort and never has been. Various belief systems have been vital to human beings in the UK from an early stage. The recent discoveries of Neolithic sites on the Isles of Orkney show just how sophisticated belief systems were many centuries ago.

Everybody has beliefs. Most human beings at some stage ask the "why" questions as to where we come from, what we are doing here and where we are going to. As Cook, Powell and Sims point out, the professions taking a purely mechanistic view is simply inadequate.[40] And in a society where we have been conned into thinking that consumerist individualism is the height of civilisation,[41] and found that notion in fact to be a sham and a trap, the concepts of community, solidarity and altruism are ever more important. Increasingly, people want to find the spiritual dimension (however we define that) built into health and social care.[42]

In America, Robert Putnam and colleagues found that Americans who were members of a faith community are better neighbours than secular Americans – more generous with their time and more positive in civil engagement.[43] If the UK is to survive and strive it needs to bring the spirit and a sense of genuine community back into health and social care.

---

[40] Cook, Powell and Sims, *Psychiatry*.

[41] Rand, *Virtue*.

[42] Mary Ellen Coyte, Peter Gilbert and Vicky Nicholls eds. (2007) *Spirituality, Values and Mental Health: Jewels for the Journey*. London: Jessica Kingsley and Peter Gilbert, "Integrating a spirited dimension into health and social care," *British Journal of Wellbeing*, Vol. 1, No. 3, June 2010.

[43] Robert Putnam and David Campbell (2010) *American Grace: How Religion Divides and Unites Us*. New York: Simon and Schuster.

Faith and Looking After the Elderly
Seeta Lakhani

Faith has a key part to play in looking after the elderly, affecting the caregiver, the recipient of care, and their loved ones. Looking after those in need of support is a universal ideal shared across all faith and belief systems, uniting people in a way that generates a greater sense of community spirit. Within the Hindu faith, the ideal of "spiritual humanism," that all human beings are essentially a manifestation of spirit, is particularly relevant in the context of care, as it encourages the practice of dignifying and divinifying humanity. There are a variety of ways that faith, and its role in elderly care, can be explored. For example, faith-sensitive care takes into account the person as a whole, catering for the things that are most important to them, especially their spiritual and religious interests. Faith's emphasis on relationship and family values help combat the isolation felt by many elderly people, and can help change current misconceptions of old age. It can also foster the development of community and broader social networks, which improve not only mental and emotional wellbeing, but have a hugely positive effect on physical health. Care givers are essential in providing genuine and heartfelt care and support, but also benefit in the process, as engaging in simple discussion on spiritual matters with an elderly client enables them to explore their own beliefs, drawing strength from their own faith when dealing with hardship and difficulty in both their personal and professional lives. Faith-based discussion can also have a transformational effect on the elderly, for whom spiritual matters are of real concern, as they search for meaning and reflect on their lives. One of the key findings is that, although providing someone with care may on the surface appear to be very ordinary, when done with heart it can have an extraordinary effect on the individual, enhancing their quality of life for the better.

Faith-sensitive care

Whether the elderly care user suffers from terminal illness, or simply requires help with the demands of daily routines which may become more difficult with age, having this extra help can provide a real opportunity for the elderly to spend more time on the things that are most important to them, including participating in hobbies and activities that they have always loved, and practicing their faith. As they are no longer anxious over having their domestic chores and daily routines maintained, the elderly can then focus their time on the things that really matter to them, giving them a greater sense of contentment and happiness. For example, one of Peepal Care's clients is a ninety seven year old lady who has trouble with her vision, and can no longer sustain her passion for reading, particularly from the Bible and other mystical books which she loves.[1] With one of our care workers taking time to read to her from her favourite books, she says she feels more peaceful and content. In this way, elderly people can benefit from the support of their care worker, not only in helping them maintain their routines, but in supporting their spiritual and religious beliefs, which can range from participating in readings to having active involvement in a religious community, which may not have otherwise been possible.

As well as supporting elderly clients in participating in the activities they love, simply being there for patients, listening to their concerns, empathising and responding is therapeutic when it comes to meeting the needs of the human spirit: the need for love and relatedness, meaning and purpose, and hope. Although some care workers and elderly care users are happy to openly discuss faith matters, there can be potential stumbling blocks to developing the level of trust required, which may include social, religious or cultural discordance, inappropriateness, judgment or proselytising. If there are such clashes, one way around this may be to avoid religion, and instead share common humanity – a "spirit to spirit" relationship. A "spirit to spirit" framework for spiritual care giving respects individuality, and can be achieved in the way care is given, by focusing on presence, journeying together, listening, connecting, creating openings, and engaging in reciprocal sharing.

Whatever perspective an individual may bring to the conversation regarding spirituality and health, the particular relevance of faith for

---

[1] Peepal Care is a domiciliary care agency, established in May 2012.

many elderly patients compels professionals to a focused consideration of this issue. As with all other aspects of health and social care, providing quality care in this dimension requires professionals to continually increase their knowledge and develop their skills, for example by attending ongoing education courses and workshops, reading relevant literature, interacting with colleagues and liaising with hospital chaplains which can all increase awareness of spiritual needs and the ability to integrate spiritual care into health and social care practice.

This is critical in providing faith-sensitive care, particularly as many patients who might otherwise have ambivalence regarding the place of spirituality in their lives have a heightened sense of concern regarding spiritual matters when faced with a life limiting illness for example. Ehman et al surveyed adult patients as to whether upon being "gravely ill" they would want to have their care professionals ask about spiritual or religious beliefs.[2] Two thirds of respondents in their sample were in favour of faith-sensitive care, and stated they would value a health or social care professional asking about their religious beliefs, and noted that a professional's inquiry regarding their spiritual beliefs would increase their trust in them. It is therefore the responsibility of health and social care professionals to learn how to provide such spiritual care for their patients, and develop their own abilities and sensitivities about spiritual issues in end of life care.

Relationship-building and family involvement

For time immemorial, the dream has always been to have a long and happy life. Those people who stood the test of time were respected as sages and seen as a source for good advice, and thanks to the progress of medicine, hygiene and nutrition, the dream of a long life has become a more widespread reality. It is, however, not always a happy reality. In a globalising trend to identify value primarily in terms of economics, old age easily becomes seen as a lack of productivity. Pension schemes can become a threat to a company's viability instead of the repayment for an employee's investment in long years of service. Those who are at present the younger pensioners, enjoying good health and assured incomes,

---

[2] John Ehman et al., "Patient Attitudes Concerning Physician Enquiry About Spiritual/Religious Beliefs," University of Pennsylvania Health System, accessed February 2013, http://www.uphs.upenn.edu/pastoral/resed/summary.html.

nonetheless fear the prospect of the expense of daily care in advanced old age. When aged people become dependent, many feel like a burden to society and have difficulty finding meaning in their lives. Combined with the trend of families drifting apart and living further away from each other, there is a real risk of growing isolation, which is particularly detrimental in old age. Elderly patients express worry that their presence is no longer valuable in the context of family and community life. In addition, the demands and stresses of care giving can become difficult for family members to manage and, on occasion, may become overwhelming, particularly when they have a number of other responsibilities to balance, including the competing demands from work, and other family and social obligations, which can leave them without the time and energy to meet all these responsibilities.

Care giving is a job, with tasks, responsibilities and the potential for stresses and rewards, which is why there is a growing need for care agencies to take up this role. However, this should not be seen as an excuse to cut families out of the picture. Rather than being considered a replacement for family support, care agencies should support family involvement in a way that can strengthen family relationships, encouraging relatives to work together to find the best possible care solutions for their elderly. Faith, and the key family values it promotes, can play a significant role in advocating this need. Greater family involvement means that rather than feeling left behind, the elderly are able to continue to feel part of family and community life. Professionals working with family members can support them to experience the positive opportunities care giving offers, fulfilling a sense of obligation and returning the affection and caring they may have received over the years.

Relatives of the elderly are sometimes not aware of the difference they can make, as they are able to inform care agencies of their elderly relative's sometimes very specific needs, preferences and routines, particularly if the care user has difficulty with communication, or prefers expressing their requirements to those they are closest to. There is a huge benefit to relatives of the elderly having greater involvement in elderly care. Not only are agencies better able to adjust the care package to very individual requirements, but families are brought closer together. Whether they live far away or close by, family members who are involved in care for their elderly have more reason to speak to each other regularly, visit more frequently, and consequently be more involved in each other's lives. Rather than being left adrift to be cared for by impersonal institutions, the elderly would far prefer having links with their loved ones involved in their care. There is an element of greater dignity and wellbeing in the elderly having a network of loved ones who, even though they may not be able to physically provide care themselves, are always there looking out for them. This ties in extremely well with Hindu teachings which emphasise the importance of maintaining the family unit, suggesting that the elderly should be cared for by families wherever possible, rather than by government institutions.

Community and social networks

As well as bringing families together, religious beliefs and practices also foster the development of community and broader social networks. For those who start becoming less mobile with age, there is a very real risk that they are less able to participate in community activities, and grow increasingly more isolated. Having the added help of a care giver can therefore really support the elderly in maintaining an active lifestyle, feeling part of the community and drawing a sense of meaning and purpose from their lives. From a health perspective, increased social contact for the elderly increases the likelihood that disease will be detected early, and that elderly people will comply with treatment regiments because members of the community interact with them, and ask them questions about their health and medical care. Elderly people who have such community networks are less likely to neglect themselves, which is why care giving, and supporting and encouraging the involvement of the elderly in faith and community, can be so critical. Many elderly people report that religion is the most important factor enabling them to cope with physical health problems and life stresses, including, for example, declining financial resources, or the loss of a spouse or partner. In a study by the National Consensus Project, 93% of elderly patients relied on religion, and a network of individuals from faith groups, when coping with health problems and difficult social circumstances.[3] Having a network of loved ones around an individual helps them to maintain a hopeful, positive attitude about the future,

---

[3] Mounica Vallurupalli et al., "The Role of Spirituality and Religious Coping in the Quality of Life of Patients with Advanced Cancer Receiving Palliative Radiation Therapy," in *The Journal of Supportive Oncology*, Vol. 10 No. 2, March/April 2012.

enabling them to cope with physical, social and emotional struggles and remain motivated to recover.

People who are linked with faith and community networks are therefore less likely to develop depression and anxiety than those who do not. Active involvement in a religious community correlates with better maintained physical health, more exercise, increased social contacts, and a longer life. Better mental health can significantly improve physical health because depression and anxiety may aggravate coronary artery disease, hypertension, stroke and other disorders. Some religious groups advocate behaviours that enhance health, such as avoidance of tobacco and heavy alcohol use. Individuals who participate in such groups would therefore be less likely to develop substance-related disorders and live longer than the general population. Faith-based organisations can therefore help to fill the gap for social services that public agencies are unable to provide to older adults. Faith-based organisations, and relationships that develop as a result of involvement, provide a natural means to foster and support care giving. Faith-based communities have regular contact with the people who need them and are likely to reflect the traditions and values of the community residents, thus lending a sense of familiarity and comfort when seeking help and support.

Spirituality can therefore be associated with connectedness, where meaning and fulfillment may be found in loving relationships. A spiritual life can be seen as a communal life, providing opportunities for a sense of belonging. Relationships therefore constitute "being there for the patient" – sharing their space, hopes and fears, being lovingly alongside a person and helping them into whatever phase they may be entering. Care giving, particularly in a community where many individuals are at risk of isolation and live alone, can be the glue that holds a community together. Being connected with a community of loved ones supports "successful aging," enabling a lifestyle where disease and disability are minimised, physical and cognitive functioning are maintained, and social connections are sustained.

The benefit for care givers

For a care giver, regardless of their faith background, providing an elderly person with the softer, interpersonal support that can help transform their lives for the better is the ultimate objective. Many care givers we come across as part of our work at Peepal Care say that their inspiration for entering the care industry is driven by their spiritual and religious beliefs. A recent "Skills for Care" survey found that nine out of ten care workers' jobs made them happy, finding it rewarding to work with the elderly, offering them a helping hand and genuine companionship, as part of their day to day working life.[4]

Supporting an elderly client to participate in faith-related activities, and engaging in spiritual discussion with them, can prompt care givers themselves to reflect on their own beliefs and values, and the degree to which their own spiritual needs are being met. It is difficult to respond to the spiritual needs of others if care workers themselves are experiencing unresolved spiritual concerns or distress. Sometimes they would need to seek out help and support for themselves so that they are more able to help others. Adhering to a belief system can empower care workers to become more able to cope with the stresses of care giving, particularly when dealing with patients with Alzheimer's disease or terminal cancer for example. Religion and spirituality's positive effects have therefore been identified as contributing to a care giver's sense of wellbeing and coping. Not only are they themselves more able to remain robust in times of difficulty and hardship, but can offer the individual, who may be undergoing tremendous suffering, heartfelt and genuine support and companionship in their time of need.

The search for meaning

A Nuffield study drew on a sample of SAGA magazine readers to elicit strength of belief, source of meaning and self-esteem in life, mental and physical health, life attitudes and a history of their religious journey.[5] Analysis of their responses indicated that those who expressed a decreased sense of personal meaning had increased levels of depression. The care giver's role is therefore to find ways to help the individual maintain their link to religious, spiritual and community practices, enabling them to find or create meaning in the later stages of their lives. The goal is to help the person establish significance and purpose,

[4] 2007 National Survey of Care Workers by Skills for Care, accessed February 2013, http://www.skillsforcare.org.uk/research/research_reports/national_survey_of_care_worke rs_2007.aspx
[5] The Leveson Centre for the study of Ageing, Spirituality and Social Policy, *Leveson Newsletter*, Issue 14, November 2005.

through processes that include social interaction, remembering and recounting the individual's spiritual journey, developing appreciation and finding hope.

We have already seen that, in some cases, patients are isolated and unable to maintain important social links. However there is also a real risk of patients falling into a cycle of loneliness to the point where this kind of social contact no longer seems desirable to them. An effective way for the care giver to open the conversation is to connect their own experience with that of the care users, letting them know they are willing to talk about spiritual concerns. Many elderly care users believe their care givers are not interested in this aspect of their lives, but by simply drawing out meaning from reminiscing about their past, for example, they are able to contribute to the emotional and spiritual wellbeing of the care user. It can also involve reassessing priorities, finding ways to address the things that interfere with the individual's ability to cherish each day, and reminding them that their prayers and thoughts can go a long way in supporting their friends and family. No matter what the beliefs of the care user or the care giver, taking time out of the day to think about the meaning of life, and exploring ways to offer emotional comfort and support, can significantly enhance quality of life for the better.

Finding meaning has also come to be regarded as a central feature of spirituality, with the impact of illness being seen as a journey to discover the hidden mysteries of life. Transcending the pain as a way of going beyond the usual limits of human experience prompts questions about the existence of a creator and possibility of life after death. It can also involve searching for meanings in situations in the context of their life experiences and moral framework. One of the most beneficial qualities of a care giver is therefore acceptance and non-judgmental compassion. Care givers need to recognise that among patients drawn from pluralistic societies, there are a variety of spiritual explorations, interpretations and expressions. An appreciation of this is essential in providing spiritual care.

In conclusion, faith has undoubtedly positive effects on elderly care. Talking to the elderly about their faith beliefs and practices during a care visit can be hugely beneficial, particularly if the patient is under substantial physical and emotional stress, providing real comfort and solace when they most need it. Ascertaining an individual's spiritual needs can also help mobilise the necessary resources, including spiritual counseling or support groups, participation in religious activities, or social contacts from members of a religious community. Although the personal care and domestic support being offered to an elderly person may on the surface appear very ordinary, it can have an extraordinary effect on the physical, emotional and spiritual wellbeing of the care user, enabling them to feel a greater sense of fulfillment, to feel more able to cope with physical and emotional struggles, and to live longer.

Greater family involvement also supports the care givers themselves, who gain a sense of satisfaction from a job well done but also receive support and encouragement from the family and friends of the elderly care user. As highlighted by the Care Giving Foundation, receiving emotional support from family and friends of the elderly care user provides an important buffer against the stress of care giving. It is the social contact, more than any tangible care they may provide, that is important. Sharing information about the elderly care user's condition can help to strengthen family participation, and the use of professionals including doctors and nurses to draw the family into more supportive positions can also be effective.

Authentic spiritual care has the effect of nourishing above all a sense of dignity, both in the elderly and in those who interact with them. But unlike most other forms of care its success cannot easily be measured. It does not fit well into the "tick-box" mentality and is not effectively enhanced by the use of external targets. There has been a lot of talk about a "compassion index" that would rate medical practitioners based on the levels of care and empathy they provided. The truth is that compassion cannot be "professionalised" or monitored or indexed; there might be behaviour that fits the definition, but it will not necessarily be motivated by "compassion." We are dealing with human beings, and human beings always need something more than a technically correct cure. They are in need of humanity; they need care for their hearts.

Faith, Values and Community Well-being
Sonia Douek

The World Health Organisation (October 2011) describes well-being as "a state in which every individual realises his or her own potential, can cope with the normal stresses of life, can work productively and fruitfully, and is able to make a contribution to her or his community."

This definition is as equally applicable to a community as a whole as it is to the individuals that make up that community. It is not possible for a community to be a healthy one if the individuals within it feel isolated, sidelined or useless.

With a move in service provision from outputs to outcomes, community well-being indicators continue to be developed. Indicators to measure community well-being "provide a concrete focus to engage local citizens and strengthen communities in discussions about what matters to them."[1] This process of developing community well-being indicators helps to inform and involve local people and organisations to identify key issues, discuss priorities, and plan future directions for their community.

However, before we can even start to look at what makes a community a healthy one, and one whose members demonstrate well-being in their daily lives, it is important for each of us to identify what the word "community" means to us, and the community to which we feel most aligned. For many of us, community is the locality in which we live. Indeed, this is the basis for the concept of Big Society, where people join together to make their locality a better place for its population. But for others of us, community is something more personal, something that we feel a strong bond with based on history, tradition and shared values.

---

[1] http://www.communityindicators.net.au.

Community – a personal perspective

My involvement as an active member of the Jewish community goes back as far as I can remember. I was born in Sydney, Australia, where my mother had the first kosher restaurant, so before the age of five I was regularly in the midst of the community and grew up with an identity that was very much bound up with food!

Moving to the UK as a small child, I soon became part of a new but very similar Jewish community, culminating in my teens as a youth leader within the local synagogue. This carried on a family tradition, as my mother had been a youth leader for the same synagogue before she married and left for Sydney. In the words of Rabbi Julia Neuberger, when talking about volunteering and the Jewish community, volunteering and community work was definitely "in my DNA."

Over the years I ran toddlers' and children's Sabbath and festival services, as well as being a lay leader within the synagogue, sitting on numerous committees and giving much of my spare time as a working mother to my local community. Indeed, today, with children flown from the nest and the potential for spare time on my hands, I find myself drawn in and volunteering for a community well-being programme in my local synagogue community once again.

Value-based communities

Given that my day job at Jewish Care is focused on volunteering and community development, what draws me to continue to give and what have I gained and learned over at least 50 years?

To me, community means a sense of belonging. An opportunity to be among people who "get me" before I have to explain myself, people who share my values and understand where they have come from so that, although we might have healthy disagreements over how these values play out and are translated, we can still walk away as friends. A community's well-being is, for me, measured by the support that its members bring to each other and the extent to which it allows individuals to play a meaningful part in its function and purpose.

As a member of the Jewish community, my involvement has always been based on a common thread: the teachings of the Torah, and the belief that these teachings are our blueprint for how we ought to live our lives and interact with each other. My involvement with other faith-based communities has taught me that, whilst we may disagree on some fundamentals of religious practice, there is more that unites than divides us. We share similar values and our support systems have grown from a desire to, in the words of Hillel, the rabbinical founder of the Talmud, "do unto others as we would have them do to us."

This leads me to believe that the strongest and healthiest communities are built upon values that people can relate to, values that we have learnt from our parents and teachers and that we hope we can pass on to our children. With these values running through from one generation to another it is not only a healthy community that we create but one that is sustainable.

Regaining a community based on shared values

Timebanking and Edgar Cahn

Some 2,000 years after Hillel founded the Talmud, I had the privilege to meet a modern day scholar with similar viewpoints. Edgar Cahn, the founder of Timebanking in the United States, brought these values alive by seeing that harnessing people's talents and putting them to good use, not only for those who are most in need but also in the simple things that will make our lives easier and enriched, was a very good way of building community. The five core values he identified are simple:

- Everyone is an asset – we all have something to give another person, and our talents and knowledge, if used correctly, can be of benefit to someone else.

- Some work is beyond a monetary price – society no longer seems to highly value those who bring up the next generation as parents and grandparents, or those who help a stranger, putting more value on paid work. Timebanking redresses the balance and shows us that our actions towards and with others, and their consequences, cannot be quantified in monetary terms.

- Reciprocity in helping – as much as we may need another's help, we all need to feel wanted and useful and should be given the opportunity to give back.

- Social networks are necessary – humans cannot function in a vacuum. It is not the actions we crave but the meaningful conversations and connections to others that are important for us to feel that we are truly alive.

- A respect for all human beings.

Tzedakah

In traditional Judaism every individual has a role to play and their actions with another human being are judged before their actions with regard to their relationship with God. This is a powerful message, it means that we can be extremely devout, attending synagogue, praying three times a day, keeping kosher to the letter of the law and making sure we do not break any of the laws of the Sabbath, but will still not be good Jews if we do not fulfill our place in society, and the role we must play in our dealings with fellow human beings.

The concept of "tzedakah," which is often literally translated as "charity," really means righteousness, justice or fairness. Whilst we are obliged in Judaism to give a tenth of our wealth, the manner in which we give our time or money is just as important as the act of giving itself. Maimonides, the 12th century scholar, teaches that the highest form of giving is neither about giving willingly nor about giving according to personal wealth. The highest form of giving is based around empowerment, described as strengthening the hand of those in need, either by extending a loan, creating a partnership or educating someone so that they can take care of themselves.

By holding on to this concept it is easy to see how an egalitarian community can grow. Where benefactors keep in mind that helping someone to be independent is better for the individual and has sustainability, we also see that the person who receives will often feel an obligation to go on and do something for someone else.

However, for some time now, the theory has been more evident in many community and welfare systems than the practice. Whilst welfare in small local communities was based on religious teaching, the advent of the Poor Law and the emergence of the welfare state created the idea that those that have should help those who don't, and a culture of dependence emerged. Whilst those who were successful held onto the concept that they had an obligation to give, the local groups became an extension of the welfare state and lost the concept of enablement. Even when giving time as opposed to money, many volunteers continued to give because it often made them feel better that they were not in need and were still able to do things for others. There is now a very fine line in welfare organisations between those who give and those who receive, with many volunteers actually using their volunteering as a means to stay connected within a community as frailty creeps up on them. In the Jewish community, the word "tzedakah" became interchangeable with "charity," and somewhere along the line we lost sight of its true meaning. This led to a paternalistic approach towards those viewed to be "in need," either because they were poor, unwell or simply old.

Putting the soul into services

This is not to denigrate the amazing commitment and work that people of faith continue to do to help and support the weakest and most vulnerable in our communities. The volunteering programme at Jewish Care sees over 3,000 people each year giving their time and skills to enable not just those who use our services to have a better life, but also those who are paid to deliver our services too. Indeed, working for a large health and social care organisation brings me into contact with those who work paid and unpaid to make life better and more meaningful for those who are isolated within our community, and if you dig deep enough most of them draw on the values of their faith (any faith) to bring meaning to that work.

For a community programme to be more than just charity, though, we need to constantly remind ourselves of the values that underpin it. We should not just go through the motions of providing high quality care or support without ensuring that the services we provide have a soul. We can provide activities for people who are lonely, but when they come into a centre or a home we must remember that they can remain lonely because they have no meaningful interaction with another human being. We can serve nutritious food with a smile, but the person, although still eating at a table with others, can find themselves eating alone. We can easily help people to fill time but forget that the real reason they want to leave the solitude of their home is to do something useful and return home with a sense of accomplishment. People can attend religious services to be part of a congregation but make no connection with the people sitting beside them.

Applying these values for the inclusion of all ages

From a community well-being point of view, it is important for all members of that community to feel included, respected and engaged. Ghandi said that "A nation's greatness is measured by the way it treats its most vulnerable members. Women, children, the unborn and the elderly are (among) the most vulnerable." I would add, however, that we are also measured on the extent to which we see such groups as "vulnerable."

If we look back to our teaching, the Torah considers growing old a blessing. The Hebrew word "chachamim" (the wise ones) is used interchangeably with "zakeinim" (the elders) in recognition of how wisdom can only be accomplished through the experience of life. Our heroes, Abraham, Sarah, and Moses, for example, were not young but were still inspirational, and their greatest achievements came in later years.

The Jewish community has the largest percentage, pro rata, of people past retirement age of any minority group in the UK. 40% of our older people are over 65 and two years ago Jewish Care, together with a Jewish ethics organisation, ResponseAblity, embarked on a community dialogue to gain a better understanding of what it is like to age well in the Jewish community, and what we could do better. Our report, "An Agenda for Ageing Well in the Jewish Community," was the result of talking with over 500 people who were either older members of the Jewish community, or providing Jewish communal services.

The message was clear – the Jewish community does welfare well, but growing old is not just about welfare! In addition, all our innovation, energies and investment was going into youth provision and activities to encourage young people to stay connected. The community was worried for its continuity and felt that youth were a priority. If we found out what activities would keep them connected we could ensure the future of the UK Jewish community.

Many older people felt marginalised both spiritually and socially. Where there were models of good practice these were deeply rooted in the core values of faith-based communities and created opportunities for people to come together to feel part of something familiar and meaningful.

Indeed, the United Nations Resolution 46/91 for Older Persons gave a commitment to five areas: Independence, Participation, Care, Self-fulfilment and Dignity. We took these ideals and together with colleagues from a wide cross-section of the Jewish community created parallel commitments to:

- Spiritual and Emotional Well-being

- Lifelong Learning

- Active Participation and Connection

- Independence and Healthy Living

- Caring for Others

It was important not just to commit to these areas but to ensure that they were addressed and underpinned by our core values of spirituality, community, caring and being purposeful, which go further than the concept of Big Society. They take account of people's need, especially as they age, to be with those with shared histories and viewpoints. They also take account of the fact that when we are vulnerable we need to be able to connect to people without explaining who we are and what is important to us. They take account of the concept that always rescuing people disempowers them but giving someone a role makes them connect with others more quickly and keeps them connected. Finally, they take account of the importance of spirituality, but understand that often this is deeper or different from religious practice.

Spiritual and Emotional well-being

Spiritual and emotional well-being are inextricably bound up together. For those in a faith-based community the concept of spirituality is complex. There is a belief that this is the same as religious practice and ritual. That religious acts such as the last rites bring both spiritual and emotional peace might be true for some, but for others spirituality is something indefinable that brings them closer to their core beliefs and gives them emotional peace.

We know that certain actions, despite being intangible, may help people feel more at peace spiritually, whether that is the opportunity to talk to someone about their fears as they face illness or older age, or the chance to celebrate traditional festivals and rituals long since forgotten. The ability to do these things within your own community, or with people who understand the importance of history and background, is powerful and necessary. The good neighbour who does your shopping or takes you to a hospital appointment can bring you a sense of connection, but this is enhanced tenfold when they allow you to have a meaningful conversation, whether that involves you voicing fears or listening to news and gossip of others with whom you have a shared history or past.

Older people can be fearful of strangers, so whilst the idea that we can all be part of one Big Society is a lovely one the reality is that we often prefer the safety and closeness of a community that shares our values and beliefs, especially when we are feeling isolated or disconnected from the outside world.

Lifelong learning

One of the three principles of Judaism is Torah (learning), and we have already seen how, in Judaism, we are constantly taught the importance of respecting our elders and those who gain wisdom. Whilst it is important for people to have a personal commitment to their own learning, communities need to commit to providing programmes that enable people to continue learning throughout their lives.

If this is what we want to be doing as we grow older, staying connected, having purposeful activity and continuing to achieve, how does this compare with your immediate thoughts about activities for older people – are they sitting in rooms, with eager faces, learning from and teaching others, or are they in a dingy bingo hall, drinking from chipped cups and waiting to go home?

One of the strongest movements to have emerged in the Jewish world – initially in the UK, and now more internationally – is Limmud. Limmud, literally meaning "learning," is a programme that brings the ages together, where participants are both teachers and learners. The common thread is Jewish, but the subject matter can be anything from Gershwin to genocide, from rabbinically-led seminars to studying "chavruta" style. You are teamed with a partner to learn together, the emphasis being on what you want to learn not who you want to learn with. The strength of Limmud lies in the fact that its multi-generational approach offers something for everyone, delivering pure equality where everyone's opinion, involvement and interest is just as important.

Active participation and connection

Each week in the synagogue service we say a prayer that blesses those who come together to pray, build places that bring us together, look after those who are in need and take care of the members of the community. This prayer is not for the community as a whole but for those individuals within it who take on such responsibilities.

Faith-based communities have a long history of volunteering. Volunteering is a way in which people can stay connected and express their community identity. A number of reports and books are now coming to the fore, identifying not just what an organisation or its beneficiaries gain from volunteers but also the way that volunteering enables social contact, personal development, personal satisfaction, a sharing of experience or skills and, as reported by Alan Luks in his book *The Healing Power of Doing Good*, a strengthening of the immune system, as well as a speedier recovery from surgery.[2]

Volunteering is not just good for the individual, or indeed for the recipient of the volunteering, but, as we know so well at Jewish Care, it brings a vitality that enhances the work of paid staff and enriches the community or organisation within which it takes place. We only have to look at the energy and sense of well-being generated by the enormous contribution of volunteers in the Olympic Games in London to see how, when people have a shared goal and feel connected to something, the benefit of their personal involvement can be felt by more than just the immediate beneficiaries.

Rabbi Menachem Mendel Schneerson, the late Lubavitcher Rebbe (head of the Lubavitch orthodox movement) taught that "The concept of retirement simply does not exist in Judaism. From birth till our last moment, each of us is permanently enlisted in the 'God's taskforce' and should not resign our post."

It is therefore vital that we create opportunities for everyone to give something so that not only their own well-being but society as a whole benefits for the greater good. The key to creating these opportunities, though, lies in sharing a common aim, and where better to do this than

---

[2] Alan Luks with Peggy Payne (2001) *The Healing Power of Doing Good*. Bloomington: iUniverse.

in a community with shared values? The challenge for those communities is to move from a position of rescuing the most vulnerable to enabling them to rescue themselves, or give something back to their community towards a common good.

Independence and healthy living

Judaism views the body and soul as inextricably linked partners, interdependent in a joint effort to successfully negotiate life's journey. This therefore places a responsibility on us to ensure that we take good care of the receptacle of our soul by looking after our bodies and minds. Putting this into the context of the community, we need to enable our members to be active, taking responsibility for their own and others' well-being.

I said at the beginning of this chapter how my involvement in community life started through food. Each of us has our own traditions surrounding food. The recipes, smells and tastes evoke memories of our parents and many of those recipes have been handed down from one generation to another. As new knowledge comes our way about what we should and should not eat, we have adapted those recipes to take account of healthy eating.

But healthy living is much more than the food we put on our plate. It is about those we share that food with, about being active and having people to share those activities with, and about feeling that we are still useful and able to participate in the things that are familiar to us.

Faith communities play a really significant role in enabling independence and healthy living. The concept of supportive communities, originating in the United States with the Naturally Occurring Retirement Communities, came about when synagogue members were identified as living in close proximity with each other but having no interaction. These supportive communities that have been replicated across the world bring together people who share their skills with each other and support each other by, for example, cooking meals for members of the group, going to local events together as a group and keeping in touch with each other to ensure that each person feels cared for and part of their community. Whilst this does not have to be a faith-based community to work, the rhythm of community life – Sabbath meals, festival events, etc. – makes it feel natural to the participants and helps to dispel some of the fear and trepidation that those on the margin of society feel when making new links.

Care

The idea of providing care to those most vulnerable in our communities was around long before the introduction of the welfare state. Whether this care was provided by the local church or synagogue, and whether it was provided at home or to those who were destitute through famine or oppression overseas, faith-based communities have had the care of others at the forefront of their existence for thousands of years. Put simply, it is a basic tenet of faith to care for others, especially those less fortunate than ourselves.

The challenge today for these communities is that the history of providing care either through a community group or through the welfare state is very often synonymous with people in need, especially financial need. Today, however, in the western world, a new phenomenon is appearing where many people still need to be cared for but can afford to pay for that care.

Often these people are cared for by institutions or charities outside of their faith community, so the challenge to these communities is to ensure that such people still feel connected, and not abandoned by them. They may not always want faith-based services, nor may it be practicable to provide them for everyone, but the communities still need to stay connected with their members and add the special element of care that only they can give.

Despite Psalm 71:9 teaching us "Do not reject me in my old age. Do not forsake me when my strength fails," when we spoke with older people in our community they felt that, because they were receiving services from one organisation or provider, especially if they went into permanent care, their own community felt they needed nothing further from them. They were being "cared for" but their community no longer cared about them.

The benefit of care providers like Jewish Care is that they not only provide high quality care but also connect people to the traditions and practices that are familiar to them. More importantly, perhaps, they also attract community members in as volunteers to enhance that feeling of connectedness that many people lose when they are either ill or isolated in old age. The volunteers often recreate a sense of community that is based on the values that link people. These are the values that we cannot always articulate but are intrinsic to our upbringing and background.

Returning to faith-based values

None of the five areas outlined above relate specifically to old age but create a person-centred approach that will build communities in which members are valued and respected, and enabled and encouraged to flourish.

However, the real question is whether these are universal values or if they are easier or more appropriate for faith-based communities. When we produced our report, we decided that, for our community, it was important to see how Jewish values fit with our approach to community and individual well-being. If older people were feeling marginalised by others in the Jewish community, how were we to influence the community leaders and decision makers? How were we to ensure that older people, who had expressed a need to connect with others in their community, could have a voice?

We found that, by articulating the values and teachings we had been brought up with, Jewish communal leaders could relate to the messages that older people wanted us to share with them. We were speaking a common language.

To our amazement, though, this was not a language that only the Jewish community understood. We found other faith-based community leaders and policy makers felt that going back to the basics of faith values gave meaning and weight to current thinking around provision and engagement of older people.

In conclusion

It is clear that a community that marginalises a section of society is not one that has well-being at its core. Any marginalisation can become insidious and after a time it is not only those on the edges of that society that suffer. The messages that such a society give out, especially a faith-based one, are in stark contrast to the values on which that society or community is built. The contrary, of course, is a community with clearly-identified values and in which all its members are signed up to those values, allowing behaviour that damages the society or community to be challenged.

Rabbi Hillel said "Do not cut yourself off from your community and do not rely on yourself alone until the day of your death," emphasising that a community relies on the individual making connection with others to ensure the collaboration of the whole – in other words, we have both an individual and collective responsibility.

The message, therefore, is simple; whilst we worry about the next generation and whether they will stay connected to their communities, we often lose sight of the values that have held communities together for thousands of years. If we keep these values of our faith at the forefront we remind ourselves of the universal values that will enable individuals within our communities to have a better sense of well-being.

More importantly, we will create a sense of well-being for our communities that will inspire the next generation to continue to live out our values and create sustainable communities for the future.

Faith Regen Foundation and Public Service Delivery
Dr Husna Ahmad

No man is a true believer unless he desires for his brother (in humanity) that which he desires for himself. The Prophet Muhammad (pbuh)

Cooperate with one another in good deeds and do not cooperate with others in evil and bad matters. Quran (5/2)

The birth of Faith Regen Foundation

Faith Regen Foundation is a Muslim-inspired, multi-faith British charity which works with disadvantaged communities to lift them out of poverty and despair, giving individuals and their families hope for a better future through economic empowerment. Muslim values underpin the work of the foundation and we identify with the universal values which we share with all the great religions of the world.

In Islam, one of the key words used for charity is *sadaqah*, often translated and understood in relation to donating money. However, Prophet Muhammad (pbuh)[1] broadened the concept of sadaqah to include most development issues, saying, "Every Muslim has to give sadaqah." To which the people asked, "O Prophet of Allah, what about the one who has nothing?" He said, "He should work with his hands to give sadaqah." They asked again, "If he cannot find (work)?" He replied, "He should help the needy who asks for help."[2]

He also once said, "Sadaqah is prescribed for every person every day the sun rises. To administer justice between two people is sadaqah. To assist

---

[1] Muslims mark their respect for the Prophet Muhammad by, after mentions of his name, using the formula "salla'llah alayhi wa sallam – may Allah bless him and give him peace." This is usually abbreviated in Arabic and in English to saw or pbuh.

[2] *Hadith* from Sahih al-Bukhari. (In Islamic terminology, the term "hadith" refers to reports of statements or actions of Muhammad, or of his tacit approval or criticism of something said or done in his presence.)

a man upon his mount so that he may ride it is sadaqah. To place his luggage on the animal is sadaqah. To remove harm from the road is sadaqah. A good word is sadaqah. Each step taken toward prayer is sadaqah."[3] On another occasion he defined sadaqah as removing thorns, bones, and stones from the paths of people; guiding the blind; listening to the deaf until you understand them; guiding a person to his object of need if you know where it is; hurrying with the strength of your legs to one in sorrow who is appealing for help; and supporting the weak with the strength of your arms.

What is the story of Faith Regen Foundation? It is the story of an effort to promote peace and tackle negative stereotypes about Islam; it is a story about making a useful contribution to civil society in the UK; it is a story about recognising that we are all different but are all one humanity.

Faith Regen Foundation was born after 9/11 as a Muslim response to the negative stereotypes about Islam and the insular mindset among many Muslims in the UK. We had a notion in our minds of what we wished to do but little idea of how to go about it. We did not want to create an organisation for Muslims, but rather an organisation that catered for people of all faiths and beliefs. We attempted a multi-faith approach to cultivate a universal responsibility for one another which recognises the importance of both social cohesion and integration and holding firmly to faith identity. Identifying the common values among the diverse faiths and beliefs in the UK, as well as working to overcome disadvantages and barriers to progression and empowerment, is what we have been working on for the past eleven years. We believe that all successful, sophisticated economies depend for their success on human capital and we know that we can unleash the potential of all in society if we give them the opportunities, the tools, the self-belief and the confidence. The statistics are so clear and the need is so evident; the most disadvantaged communities are those that are ethnic minorities, and many turn to their faith for strength and hope.

As a charity we are a not-for-profit organisation and we apply for funding from different pots such as trusts and foundations, local government and central government departments. More recently, we have been working as a subcontractor for prime contractors, who are mostly private organisations, although a charity is our prime contractor

---

[3] Hadith from Musnad Ahmad ibn Hanbal.

on the Work Programme in London. We are an investee of the Social Investment Business and have their support in developing our financial models and business plans. We have also been able to build strong partnerships with other faith and black, Asian and minority ethnic (BAME) organisations.

Well-wishers and supporters from all faith communities, as well as different sectors such as education, employment and health, have been and continue to be attracted to the organisation because of the vision we promote. As well as the board of trustees, in the beginning we also had a special advisory panel where the various faiths of the UK were represented. We realised early on that in order to promote our vision we needed to do tangible things, we needed to show the results of our interventions – not just engage in dialogue (although it does play a crucial role, particularly interfaith dialogue). We realised we were very much about active faith in the local community.

I am surprised and delighted that we have survived over a decade. The challenges have been enormous but the rewards have been tremendous. I call it the helter skelter ride of active faith.

Benefits of faith-sensitive public service delivery

The Islamic concept of poverty alleviation is about empowerment; it is much more than just charity, it is about investment, education and lifting people out of impoverishment. The need, therefore, is for investment in education, communication and skills and vocational training to help youth, women and disadvantaged people.

At the beginning of our journey we worked directly with faith institutions such as mosques, churches, gurdwaras and synagogues. This was an excellent way to engage with the faith communities in settings in which they felt comfortable and relaxed. This in turn meant better learning and progression opportunities. We were able to provide staff that spoke their language and understood the faith sensitivities of the communities. We were able to provide on-site crèches in many of our projects which really helped women from faith and ethnic-minority backgrounds to engage with our programmes. Our aim was to capacity build these institutions so that they could commence public service delivery directly, and I am pleased to say that we were successful on a number of occasions in assisting these institutions to do so. However, there have also been difficulties, mainly involving health and safety rules and bureaucracy, in terms of monitoring projects and audit trails. To circumvent these obstacles we decided to open our own centres and deliver public services directly – this would ensure that the projects complied with all the legal rules and regulations. Our links with faith centres and communities have not diminished, but we have actually built partnerships which have also enabled projects outside the realms of public service delivery to flourish and grow. We have delivered many courses from our centres over the years including:

- English for Speakers of Other Languages (ESOL)
- IT classes
- LearnDirect
- Skills for life
- National Vocational Qualifications (NVQs) in childcare,
- Customer services and IAG (Information, Advice and Guidance) training
- Advice for business start-ups and social enterprises
- Employability skills training
- Job searches
- Work placements
- Mentoring

Today we are essentially a training, skills and employment provider of public services for disadvantaged ethnic-minority and faith communities.

We have also piloted a family learning scheme from a famous fast food outlet (whose name I will not mention), which was very well received by the participants.

How do we differ from non-faith-based organisations?

I think the current position in the employment sector is leaving very little room for manoeuvre – largely because of IT security, human resources issues, CRB checks and the end-loading of payments. At Faith Regen Foundation, we are working as a subcontractor for prime contractors and have a clear remit for delivery, which makes it difficult for us to add value apart from the interaction clients have with our staff. We value and develop our staff and respect our clients or beneficiaries, because if the clients do not get respect from us how are they to feel confident to face the outside world? Interestingly, a number of the people who work for our organisation have no background in the employment or education sector (including myself), but they bring transferable skills and a belief in what we stand for. Also, the staff are from diverse faiths and ethnicities, with many of them actually being former clients.

In the past we have had additional dimensions to our delivery which have been valuable but unfunded such as providing health surgeries for clients, faith sensitive provision if required (such as women-only classes), incubation space, as well as access to our IT room for schoolchildren and women in the same building.

Government policy is something which we have engaged with keenly since our inception, as this is an area to which we can add value through the perspective of diversity, i.e. religion and race. We have held numerous seminars, conferences and roundtable discussions on a variety of topics from the Arms Trade Treaty to climate change and Peaceful Coexistence, as well as airing a TV show called Muslim Women Today on a Bangladeshi satellite show, for which we managed to get the likes of Avril McIntyre of LifeLine and Chris Grayling, the former Employment Minister, to speak on the plight of Muslim women in the labour market. We have also held a roundtable discussion at the US Embassy discussing ethnic-minority women and the labour market in the UK and US.

Challenges of public service delivery

Delivering public services as a faith-based organisation has been difficult at times, as faith has been a difficult concept to acknowledge in the public arena in the UK for a very long time. Also, changing government policies, changing Cabinets and ministers' priorities, and, finally, a change in government, have all had an impact on faith-based organisations, as well as the charity sector as a whole. What is ironic is that governments will come and go but the faith institutions are here through thick and thin. It is the churches, mosques and other faith institutions that have to bear the brunt of the bank bailouts and austerity measures that have come into force.

I think that the notion that politics and religion cannot mix is an idea inconsistent with the very foundations of our laws and ideas of morality. Religion and politics have always mixed, or, rather, spirituality and faith have always been part of the political and social fabric of any society. Our very laws here in the UK are derived from and saturated in the Judeo-Christian traditions of this nation.

The very idea that there is morality, that there is a distinction between "good" and "evil," is a clear indication of the profound impact faith has had to play in developing our sense of self and, by extension, our laws and governance. Indeed, many so-called "secular" governments still fund religious education. In America, politicians take their oaths on the Bible, and all Judeo-Christian religious events are declared national holidays, including the weekends.

The Orthodox Islamic tradition has always stipulated that belief and submission to God is an encompassing way of life; politics and the way a nation is governed naturally come under that. However, I believe there to be misconceptions of what this entails from both sides of the debate. Today, many Muslims are very much against the idea of a "secular" state. To them, it means a state in which there is no room for faith to play an integral role in the development and regulation of the country, and therefore a state in which no spiritual or moral standard is upheld or promoted. It is important to note, however, that many Muslims in the UK are diaspora communities, and are anti-secularist due to the consequences of years of colonialism and secular rule, just as many in the West are adamantly against religion playing any role in the state because of the years of bloody wars and strife that came through having a centralized religious authority in the form of the Vatican.

Today in Britain, religion is one of the equality strands which is protected and is supported by the UK government through policy, legislation and government bodies. The Equality and Human Rights Commission (EHRC) is the independent body responsible for reducing inequality, eliminating discrimination, strengthening good relations between people and protecting human rights. It is mandated to investigate and monitor human rights concerns to ensure the effectiveness of human rights enactments. The EHRC has the capacity to advance the promotion and affordability of human rights at a national level in an attempt to create a more socially-inclusive society.

The Equality Act in the UK has also been established and is a legislative framework that stipulates that no one should be discriminated against because of their age, disability, race, religion, sex or sexual orientation, and it has made any such founded discrimination illegal. Whilst Faith Regen Foundation has made alliances with, and continues to have the support of, some of the most wonderful individuals and organisations who make me feel proud to be British, as a practicing Muslim woman of Bangladeshi origin (i.e. I wear the hijab) I have over the years too often experienced a condescending attitude among funders and bureaucrats. I have seen many times that we are regarded as a tick box item for equality and diversity purposes. Our organisation has faced indirect discrimination and Islamophobia on a number of occasions, but we continue because we know that what we are doing is a much needed intervention; what we are doing is something that others are not able to provide. Although we are a charity, we are as good as any organisation in the private sector, we have a professional attitude to our delivery and our staff are trained and competent to deliver the services we are paid for. We are focused and target driven because without that we will not be taken seriously. Our track record shows our ability to deliver results but we have constantly faced challenging issues because of the uncertainty of new contracts and the loss of key staff who have been trained over years. In the past, the problem was the short-term nature of the contracts that were given out, i.e. two-year contracts. Now the new challenge is the complete overhaul of the employment sector and the introduction of initiatives like the Work Programme.

I sometimes ponder why, after running for over ten years, we have not become a much larger organisation; why is it that with successful delivery, a strong track record and an excellent reputation we are still just being thrown the crumbs? I recognise that we have been on a tremendous learning curve during the past decade and we made many mistakes along the way (and continue to make mistakes), but what surprises me is that there are other organisations out there (which are not BME organisations) that still continue to grow and win contracts despite being no better in their track record than us. Although it is frustrating – as a regular healthy turnover would help to free us up to find new initiatives to develop and support, as well as improve our current programmes – at the end of the day we are not in business to look at our size, we are in business to support the most vulnerable, and if it means doing things which are unfunded we will still continue to do so for as long as we are able. Presently, one of the voluntary roles we are playing is with A Year of Service for the Queens Diamond Jubilee, which is an initiative of the Department for Communities and Local Government. We worked with mosques during the month of Ramadan throughout the country to take part in interfaith *iftars* (breaking the fast) and the preparation of hampers for local charities. This was a huge success and meant the idea of serving the community was expounded more clearly. We have also supported Climate Week this year and will continue to do so in the next.

Volunteerism is something which is at the heart of faith communities and it needs to be embedded more strongly in our society. I am reminded, here, of the story of my grandfather who lived in South Asia and took his family to another country in the late 1930s, looking to make a life in this new place. He left his wife and young children in a village and went to the town on business for a week. During this time one of the children became very ill and died. My grandmother had no man in the house to help her to bury the child and no one from the village came to help her, so she was left alone with this dead child for a couple of days – until someone in a distant village heard what had happened and came with his sons and buried her child. When my grandfather returned he was so shocked and angered that he vowed he would leave that country and never return because there was no sense of social responsibility or good neighbourliness for someone in distress. The lesson I learnt from this story was that everyone thinks someone else will do work for the community so they don't need to, but the reality is that if we all chip in the burden will be lighter.

As the Dalai Lama has clearly enunciated, "The problems we face today, violent conflicts, destruction of nature, poverty, hunger and so on, are human-created problems which can be resolved through human effort, understanding and the development of a sense of brotherhood and sisterhood. We need to cultivate a universal responsibility for one another and the planet we share."

Way forward

Today, Faith Regen Foundation continues to work at the grassroots level to bring different community and faith groups together under the banner of sustainable development. Behind this banner, there exists an inherent belief that, no matter what our background is, we all seek the same goals, and we all hold a strong desire to leave behind a better world for our children to inhabit. We do what we do because we believe that we cannot wait for someone else to take care of our own. We all have a social responsibility as British citizens, human beings and people of faith to care for our local communities. We believe that by activating citizens to participate in British society through a variety of means – such as being part of the workforce, volunteering, or progressing through lifelong learning – we can create a society which embraces equality and diversity. All human beings are equal and therefore they all have a right to the opportunities which can enable them to provide for themselves and their families and lift them out of the vicious cycle of poverty.

Our success has been due to our faith values and deep conviction in searching for the good in everyone, knowing that we are all on the same journey, and that sometimes we need to stretch out our hands to give help to some of our companions.

Today, in order to remain sustainable, we have broadened our horizons and are operating at both a national and international level to build bridges with and between faith communities, government and civil society to stimulate greater understanding and respect for cultural and religious diversity. We use our networks with faith-based communities as well as statutory and non-statutory bodies to promote interfaith dialogue, address poverty, provide greater opportunities for employment and training to ethnic minority groups and tackle climate change.

We have two subsidiaries – I2i and Global One 2015, which are our commercial wing and international wing respectively. We are already developing manuals on maternal health in Africa, water conservation manuals for Asia, a Green Guide for the Hajj and even a cartoon on water conservation, and we have also set up offices in Somalia and Bangladesh.

However, despite these developments, the future is still uncertain. The chances of an organisation such as Faith Regen Foundation surviving are slim for two reasons: the economic climate and the lack of financial support given towards core funding of charities. Will we still be delivering public services in the future? Personally, I am not convinced that we will, because, as I have stated earlier, the direction in which the employment sector is going means there is a chance that we as a charity may lose our faith. By this I mean that we may turn into just another organisation trying to reach government targets, and therefore lose the spirit of our very existence.

Although the future may look difficult, we are people of faith, and we are hopeful and patient; we know that we can never give up. As the eternal optimist, I believe that God has a design and as long as there is a need for Faith Regen Foundation it will continue to add some value to Britain and beyond.

Changing Shape, Keeping Vision
Avril McIntyre

LifeLine Community Church was established on the borders of Redbridge and Barking and Dagenham in the 1970s, beginning simply as a group of people who based their way of life on the values practised by the first Christians. This starting point remains the basis for the activities of the church today; our primary aim is to demonstrate daily the way of life practised by the first Christians, whether at home, at work or in the neighbourhood.

In the following chapter, I will tell the story of LifeLine Projects, looking at its origin in the pioneering activities of two members of LifeLine Church and its subsequent development into a much larger service provider. I will describe the "growing pains" experienced as part of this process, and the challenges we faced as we worked to maintain our founding ethos and "solution-focused" approach to services. Finally, I will provide a picture of the current outlook for LifeLine – those areas of the community in which we are currently committed to making a difference.

The origins of LifeLine: a story of champions

The foundations for Lifeline Projects (or simply "LifeLine") were laid when, in 1998, a group of volunteers from LifeLine Community Church began responding to need in the local community. These volunteers were moved by compassion for those individuals who, despite living in the locality, were found to be isolated and without a voice, and they gave their time to helping them find a place to belong in the community. Two stories in particular represent this starting point of LCP's journey.

Meeting a need

A member of LifeLine Church was waiting for her children at the gates of a local primary school when she noticed that two Pakistani women were taking it in turns to read an English children's storybook to one another. It dawned on her that they were trying to improve their English, and they seemed to be struggling, so she offered to help.

The two women enjoyed her support so she invited them to come to her house once a week to work on their English in a more relaxed setting, at which point she enlisted the help of other volunteers from the church.

The English language "classes" that the volunteers offered were very informal and social occasions. They were focused primarily on developing everyday communication skills, and the activities were designed to be enjoyable and non-threatening. For example, the volunteers would use everyday objects to help individuals improve their vocabulary and conversational skills.

Over the coming months, the two original volunteers began to bring other women to the weekly sessions and the group grew until 12 women from four different countries were coming along with their children. This increase in demand meant that the volunteers began to source alternative venues for the classes; before long, sessions were being held in a classroom in a local school and then in the hall of another local church.

Listening ears

At the same time as this, another woman from LifeLine Church was listening to a radio discussion regarding young people and sexual health information. She felt compelled to phone in to the radio station and challenge the presenters that the focus seemed to be on adults presenting information to young people in a one-way stream, with no-one actually listening to the young people themselves.

On the back of this, she decided to establish a "listening" programme which she called EARS. She went part-time at work, and began going into schools to meet with students during lunchtimes, finding the schools to be very open to what she was doing. These weekly drop-in sessions quickly gathered momentum, even though all she was doing was simply listening. Students of any age or background would come and share their issues; if they asked, she would pass on information to them, but really her job was just to listen. The problems she encountered were wide ranging: from a student letting her know that their goldfish had died that morning and that they were finding it difficult to get over it, to young people struggling with eating disorders.

As she grew more connected with schools and the local authority, more requests for training and support came through. There was a demand for extra support for certain students in transition years (going from year 6 to 7) for example, as well as training on subjects such as self-esteem.

Building a framework

In 2000, LifeLine Projects was born to formalise and grow the grassroots initiatives that had already been established by these volunteers.

The organisation, now more widely known as "LifeLine," made a decision early on that it would operate according to values of justice, compassion and integrity. We adopted the term "faith inspired" to describe the motivational basis of the organisation, and put no restrictions on employees and beneficiaries according to their own faith. We did not want the limitations that the term "faith-based organisation" might bring, and wanted to avoid being put into a box by the local authority.

A recent visitor to our offices asked the question of one of our employees, "If LifeLine emerged from the activities of a church, how does this affect the day-to-day running of services?" The truth is, our church-based origins do not leave a significant *tangible* imprint on the work we carry out daily. But what they have given us is a clear faith ethos, a set of values that now form a foundation for everything we do. Our staff understand this, whether or not they have a personal faith themselves, and, by extension, each member of staff is a champion of our ethos.

Perhaps one way in which LifeLine Church maintains a ongoing conversation with its charitable wing is through the influence of Trustees. I have always made sure that there is a representation of LifeLine Church members on our Board – these individuals are able to ensure that the faith values upon which we are built are never compromised.

"You don't know what you don't know"

With the groundwork laid, and a clear vision in place regarding the kinds of solutions it wanted to provide in the community, LifeLine swiftly learnt the importance of looking beyond its own pool of talent and drawing in advice from "allies." When a local college offered to train ESOL teachers and pay for a crèche, we thought it was a generous partnership until one of our allies realised that the college was actually making a significant amount of money from the agreement. This ally began working closely with us to offer further direction and support.

The early days of LifeLine's development, as illustrated vividly by the above story, brought with them many learning opportunities. We came to realise that, quite simply, "you don't know what you don't know." The college in question was more savvy than us when it came to delivering services, and we benefited greatly from the advice of organisations further down the road than we were; people who could show us the ropes of statutory funding, who knew as much as the college did. For organisations in their inception, and indeed at any stage in their development, asking for help is key. It's not about exposing your own naivety or lack of knowledge, but drawing upon the expertise of others – those who are already doing what you would like to be doing. As an organisation, we hope to be continually learning through this extremely simple process of asking for help. In our experience, those we have approached for assistance have been more than happy to offer it.

Solution-focused delivery: maintaining a vision

Over the years, LifeLine continued to diversify the types of training it provided in order to meet emerging demand and need in the local community. For example, in 2003 we secured contracts from Learn Direct and a Local Further Education College to provide a range of training in IT skills, ESOL and Childcare. All of these were delivered according to a "solution-focused approach"; often we found that we were the only ones around the table locally that were focused on finding what we could do to overcome problems, rather than simply pointing out the apparent lack of solutions. We continued to work closely with the borough and funders to provide such responses to the common problems that we found in Barking and Dagenham and other local authorities.

Until 2004, LifeLine had approximately 40 staff, and was a modest East London-based charity. Throughout the course of that year, however, we secured five European Social Fund contracts directed towards training needs other than ESOL, such as IT, Family Learning and Information, Advice and Guidance. This meant that LifeLine's turnover increased by 10 times in that short period. During this pressured phase recruitment was a bit "hit and miss," and employees received only a limited induction process. The organisation, it would be fair to say, struggled with the rate of change, and with the lack of a clear vision across all departments, as well as inexperienced management, performance became patchy. It was felt that the organisation did not represent excellence in what it was delivering.

In 2007, LifeLine regrouped and focused on returning to the original ethos and culture it had in the early days. This involved redefining the vision and values of the organisation from within. There was a further investment, for example, in a number of "staff days," designed to bring the organisation as a whole back to its core mission, and on top of this the recruitment process was given a particular overhaul, with recruiters looking for the right people (with the right attitude) as well as those who had the skills for the job.

Over time, this strategy has enabled LifeLine to develop a comprehensive model of support that aims to meet the needs of the "whole" individual, in the context of his or her family and community. There is a particular focus on the social, health, economic and relationship issues that can act as barriers in people's lives.

A new season

Over the past twelve years, LifeLine has developed an effective and innovative outreach model that proactively engages people who would otherwise be unlikely to seek out support. This model recognises the diverse range of barriers that such individuals face and takes its programmes into accessible, ward-level community venues such as schools, libraries, children's centres, GP surgeries and Housing Associations. The focus is on the whole person, recognising that lasting change does not happen through one isolated intervention or programme.

In addition, LifeLine adopts a "no wrong door" approach where anyone who accesses any part of its delivery is able to connect with a range of support to suit them. This facilitates strong referral mechanisms both internally and externally as project teams liaise closely with other departments internally and build strong partnerships externally on a day-to-day basis to meet the "whole person" needs of our beneficiaries. LifeLine is now engaging 5% of the Barking and Dagenham population on an annual basis, and has an average annual turnover of £4.4 million.

Our work is focused on 3 areas, still reflecting the original goals and focus of the charity:

- *Youth* – engaging young people who are struggling or have failed in the education system and enabling them to reengage in a meaningful way;

- *Employment and skills* – re-engaging unemployed adults in sustainable employment; and

- *Families* – supporting parents to become confident and positive in their role, developing strong, resilient families.

LifeLine has delivered in excess of £20million of public sector contracts since 2005. Here is a more detailed look at the various services on offer.

LifeLine's services

Youth

As part of its youth strategy, LifeLine runs an alternative school known as "LifeLine Institute." Funded by the London Borough of Barking and Dagenham, the Institute offers opportunities for young people who would have been in Year 11 but are not in education for a variety of reasons, ranging from permanent exclusion to having recently arrived from overseas. Engage is a similar programme, funded by Havering, which seeks to reengage young people who have been excluded from all other education provision.

LifeLine is also on the framework for alternative schools provision in the London Boroughs of Hackney and Croydon.

"VIP" mentoring is a programme offered by LifeLine, and funded by various sources, which involves working in partnership with schools to support young people at risk of becoming NEET (Not in Education, Employment or Training). It has been delivered for the past 11 years, and works in a complimentary way with existing school pastoral support. LifeLine mentors will meet regularly with students, identified by their school as being at risk of referral to alternative provision, and get alongside them, taking time to listen to their concerns and offer advice and encouragement. The scheme aims to instill these young people with a clear sense of *Vision, Identity* and *Purpose* for their lives – core values which, we believe, will help them walk into their future with confidence, self-awareness and a clear sense of direction. Findings show a 93% reduction in reports of incidents for those mentored students, as well as 58% improved attendance.

Employment and Training

LifeLine is working as a sub-contractor for A4e to deliver the Work Programme in Barking and Dagenham, Redbridge and Havering. This entails an intensive two-year intervention which not only enables people to gain work but supports them to sustain employment.

The "Moving On" programme for ex-offenders offers support and training to empower those in custody or recently released to gain employment and tackle the multiple barriers they often face when re-entering the community.

LifeLine also provides Matrix-accredited information, advice and guidance (funded by National Careers Service), enabling clients to make decisions on learning, training and work opportunities in a confidential and helpful environment.

Our job brokerage service is funded by Job Creation Partnerships and covers five Local Authorities. We offer highly effective one-to-one support to enable people to gain employment.

Children's Centres and Families

LifeLine is currently the lead agency in Croydon for providing evidence-based parenting programmes for targeted families across the borough. To do this, we are funded by the London Borough of Croydon.

We also offer our own bespoke antenatal education for two Primary Care Trusts, engaging 800 first-time mothers each year. In addition, we offer breastfeeding peer support in maternity wards, baby clinics and Children's Centres in the boroughs of Barking and Dagenham and Havering.

Key advice

LifeLine's journey has been long and rewarding, but also greatly challenging. We have had many successes along the way, yet have also encountered difficulties and made a number of mistakes. As a result, we have learned a lot, and we are eager to pass on this knowledge to similar faith-based organisations looking to get involved in providing solutions to their local communities. To organisations in this position I would give the following advice:

- Know your strengths. There are multiple "needs" to be met, but it is important to pursue areas where you can bring something of real value. LifeLine's strength was its passion for and ability in training and equipping, particularly around family and relationships. Much of what we have developed over the years has been based around this.

- Invest in spending time finding those with the right skills but also the right heart – both are critical.

- Hearing God is a process; providing a service to your community is a journey and you will not get all the answers at once.

- Recently, LifeLine has turned down a number of contract opportunities and made some radical decisions in line with our core mission and focus. We have made mistakes in the past which have taken us "off mission," so we are always prepared to take time to process and plan, to seek advice, and to make difficult choices, if necessary, to maintain this aim.

- Focus on solutions, and seek partnership where appropriate. Take time to work with other people locally, understand the issues facing the community, local authority and partners and work with them to find solutions.

- There is a new opportunity to re-shape what is happening locally; the welfare state is breaking down and the church has to step into the gap and make the difference.

To Conclude

I have hoped to provide an overview, here, of LifeLine's origins in the initiatives of two faith-inspired volunteers, as well as the process of our expansion into the organisation we are today. I have also looked at what it means for a faith-inspired organisation like LifeLine to undergo significant changes to its size, shape and structure, asking how, in the midst of this restructuring, it might preserve its core vision. The decision, in 2007, to regroup and re-establish our ethos was key, I think, to the development of our charitable identity.

A quality mark inspector recently commented that every LifeLine employee she had spoken to could clearly articulate the values of the organisation, which indeed suggests we have been successful in embedding our ethos. But is this enough? Perhaps not. Looking at the journey we have taken, there are many things along the way that I feel we could have done differently, and we have certainly not achieved all we would have liked. Yet, in spite of this, we are still making a difference both to our locality and to the shape of voluntary-sector service provision. If we are able to reach thousands of individuals yearly, then we can make a significant difference to the lives of hundreds. Looking to the future, this is the legacy upon which we would like to build.

A Citizen's Right to Shape the Public Imagination
Raheel Mohammed

The power of stories and public ownership over these stories is an idea that can be found all over the world and across many centuries. Storytellers do not simply excite or provoke our imagination but they trace an outline of future possibilities. Their words become a catalyst for future generations.

This public imagination is complex and made up of contributions from all communities. Both religion and art lend themselves to this complexity and communal effort. They both deal in metaphor and an understanding of the world that does not have to be fully grasped but intuitively realised. They both rely on people as observers and participants.

In this chapter I will argue that having a myriad of public voices and ideas in the social ether is important, perhaps more than ever before. Through my work in Maslaha, a social enterprise, I will show how our practical work is driven by a communal imagination in dealing with some of our most pressing issues. The chapter will illustrate how Maslaha follows in a long tradition of using metaphor and artistic/religious language to tackle social needs and provide fresh perspectives and opportunity in moments of crisis.

Public language

Take Gaudi's iconic church in Barcelona, the Sagrada Familia, built "for the people by the people," the first stone laid down in 1882. Made possible by the donations of worshippers, the church remains unfinished and still relies on public donations. It continues to be built in the public gaze, and as generations of visitors marvel at its construction they too become a part of the Sagrada Familia's story.

There is a kind of vulnerability in watching this artistic and religious endeavour continue to evolve and take shape. Once you have visited the church and seen the bulldozers inside, and heard the sound of hammering and drilling, you can't help but feel a part of its history.

The Sagrada Familia is an example of how religion and art have sculpted and influenced the public imagination for centuries, helping to widen the language of what it means to live in a particular society at a particular time. This widening of language has been an integral part of Maslaha's work, whether it is creating health resources, tackling stereotypes about Muslim women, or exploring the exchange of ideas between Islam and Europe through our exhibitions.

Our health resources at Maslaha (www.caringforyourheart.org), for example, combine faith and medical information. They are not only used in GP surgeries and hospitals but also in libraries, internet cafes, community centres and schools in Birmingham and London. Our work permeates into everyday environments, so that the resources become an organic process. Our health resources use film, calligraphy, the Azan, or call to prayer, and animation to help reinforce health messages, while creating a new vocabulary for health or any other area of our work.

Sound and oral tradition have always been a central part of Islam, and the Azan, a powerful utterance, has been central to the lives of Muslims for centuries. In fact, the first word of the Quran revealed to the Prophet Muhammad (pbuh) was "Recite." We have used this aural heritage to tackle pressing social issues, for instance using the Azan in some of our films tackling diabetes as a way of grabbing the attention of different communities we have worked with in London. The unexpected use of a religious sound with a health message has worked with surprisingly good results, creating a sort of creative dissonance that requires a different perspective on a particular problem or issue.

The 2010 Turner prize winner, Susan Philipsz, recreated a sound installation with three versions of a Scottish lament, Lowlands Away. As well as playing in Tate Britain it was originally played beneath three bridges over the River Clyde in Glasgow. Philipsz has talked about sound as being a form of sculpture and the significance and presence of the human voice in societies before there was heavy machinery and cars. Her work transmits the ancient rhythms of the past into the present, suddenly anchoring an environment into a history that has probably been forgotten but should be remembered. The walls between the past and present are suddenly porous and the cities of yesterday reappear.

It is this temporal fracture, the past suddenly heard in the present, that can be powerful and suddenly provide a new perspective, as with the Azan in our health resources. If we are asking people to change their behaviour, whether it is in health or anything else, shouldn't those messages be beautiful, and work on both an emotional and spiritual level?

Artwork of any kind is not passive, whether it is sung, written, sculpted, or painted. It can seep into our DNA with the first contact, knowingly or not. The effect can be immediate or remain dormant for years until a spark of inspiration releases the idea.

Artistic and religious images and ideas can be wild, and sometimes buildings are not strong enough to contain these ideas. In such cases, they spill out onto the streets, clinging to the air, and to your skin and clothes, and there is no way of shaking them off.

Our I Can Be She project involves working with young Muslim women in East London, with the aim of empowering participants to express themselves in new creative ways through radio, photography, film and fine art.[1] As part of this project these young women have exhibited their work in a public gallery and worked with the South Bank Centre to produce a 20-minute Bollywood film. Instead of being talked about through the narrow lens of the "hijab," these young women are expressing themselves on their own terms. Their photographs are powerful, authentic and not at all contrived.

Their public expression, through the exhibition of their work, adds new language and metaphor to the discourse around Muslims and Islam. The importance of broadening language crops up in George Orwell's novel, *Nineteen Eighty-Four*. A character called Syme talks enthusiastically about getting rid of verbs and adjectives so that thought crime is no longer possible. We need more vocabulary, and religion and art are important and much-needed tools to challenge established ideas.

The workshops run through our I Can Be She project are not simply about learning how to use a camera but are a way of exploring identity, what it means to live in Britain today and what it means to be a Muslim in Britain today.

---

[1] See the website, www.icanbeshe.org.

You can understand why the writer and film-maker Iain Sinclair wrote in his book *Lights Out for the Territory*:

> The city is the subject, a fiction that anyone can lay claim to. "We are all artists," they used to cry in the Sixties. Now, for the price of an aerosol, it's true. Pick your view and sign it. Sign events that have not yet happened.[2]

This idea of re-imagining the public space and reclaiming it is a theme that runs strongly through our City Speaks exhibition produced in partnership with the British Council. There are two strong examples of artists in the exhibition who literally paint the landscape with the voices and faces of those communities that reside there.

American artist Candy Chang, and the Civic Centre which she co-founded in New Orleans, engages citizens in dialogue with their city. Chang has taken her work across the US, to Kazakhstan, the Netherlands, The Azores, Mexico, Portugal and Finland. Projects include stickers that help residents voice how they want city spaces to be used; a Finnish underpass that has been transformed into a reflection on career choices; and an online tool which helps people influence the development of their neighbourhoods.

One of her projects, *Before I Die*, is an exercise in inspiration, a wall of dreams. You are walking along the street when you suddenly encounter a black wall which fills an abandoned shop front with the statement at the top: *Before I Die*. The wall is filled with white lines, some of which have had responses chalked on each line: "Write a book," "learn a second language," "see all homeless people with homes," "see my students become teachers." And so you stop and reach for the chalk…

Chang's Civic Centre works with academic institutions, community organisations, public schools and government to allow communities to give their input into how they would improve their neighbourhoods, make living in the city easier to navigate, and use public space to insert a creative step into each day.

For French artist JR the city comes alive with the faces of the people who live in it. He has taken this literally, pasting faces on the rooftops of Kenyan slums. Similarly, in Brazil, you look at the favela from a distance and all you can see are its inhabitants looking back at you from the

---

[2] Iain Sinclair (2003) *Lights Out for the Territory*. London: Penguin, p. 2.

hillside. JR has also taken images of the youth of the French banlieues (suburbs) pulling comically scary faces and pasted their photographs in the bourgeois neighbourhoods of Paris, in response to the fear and demonisation of these young people. He has also pasted the faces of Israelis and Palestinians side by side on the barrier that separates them. In *Women are Heroes*, JR turns his focus to women who are victims of conflict, war, violence and oppression.

With these giant images, the community reclaims the streets, the faces of the unheard voices conquer the walls and thus their stories begin to be told. In order to hear these stories, JR engages closely with each community, gaining their confidence enough to capture their faces on camera, full of expression.

At a recent lecture he said:

> What we see changes who we are. When we act together, the whole thing is much more than the sum of the parts. So I hope that, together, we'll create something that the world will remember. And this starts right now and depends on you.[3]

Religion and art

But perhaps the way religion and art have worked together in the past provide clues to what could develop in the future. In the examples below we have attempted to understand the divine enmeshed in public life in different social, political and cultural contexts.

The prolific Ottoman architect Sinan, who was widely known as the Turkish Michelangelo, was responsible for many buildings that fill the Istanbul skyline. Of course his primary aim was to create magnificent architecture but praising the divine also appears to be an important element of his work. In his biography, Sinan's domed mosques are described as microcosmic representations of the universe:

---

[3] JR, "JR's TED Prize wish: Use art to turn the world inside out," a lecture for TED, March 2011, accessed February 2013, http://www.ted.com/talks/jr_s_ted_prize_wish_use_art_to_turn_the_world_inside_out.htm l.

Columns and minarets are like cypresses, marbles with wavy patterns like oceans, arches with alternating voussoirs soaring to the heavens in the manner of rainbows, small bubble-like domes are like bubbles on the surface of the sea of pleasure, great domes like mountains carved out from the earth, cupolas are suspended in the manner of heavenly spheres, interior spaces and fountain courtyards are like paradisiacal gardens.[4]

In the streets of Rome a young artist by the name of Caravaggio (1571-1610), was pioneering a new form of artistic expression, a heightened naturalism. As he became embroiled in street fights at night, his days were spent experimenting with his paintings. Commissioned to produce a number of works depicting biblical stories, he began using real life models to depict these religious scenes. The effect was to suddenly make very modern these centuries-old Christian stories in paintings such as the *Calling of St Matthew*. This form of naturalism was designed to bring the religious hurtling into the contemporary public space.

During Caravaggio's lifetime Naples was the second largest city in Europe after Paris, with a population of around 300,000. A colony of Spain at the time, Naples would be suited to Caravaggio's life and his art, both of which were executed at full throttle. It was also a city wracked with mass unemployment, poverty and a lack of housing.

Caravaggio escaped to Naples in 1606 after killing a man in Rome over a tennis match, but it would be in this city, divided by "religion and wickedness," that he would paint arguably one of the greatest religious paintings of the 17th century, the *Seven Acts of Mercy*, for the church Chiesa del Pio Monte della Misericordia. The church was led by a religious order devoted to hands-on charity and tackling the urban crises affecting Naples.

In this painting, a street in Naples portrays the afflictions of the world and a moment of salvation for those affected by the brutal existence of life. Religious paintings such as these were a significant part of the cityscape, allowing a public conversation with the divine and providing comfort to citizens of the city.

Hagia Sophia, the 6th-century Emperor Justinian's imperial church, would be transformed into a mosque by Sultan Mehmed in 1453 after the

---

[4] Gulru Necipoglu (2005) *The Age of Sinan, Architectural Culture in the Ottoman Empire.* London: Reaktion Books.

conquest of Constantinople by the Ottomans. It is reported that when the Sultan first entered the church he was in awe of the interior design. According to the 19th century chronicler Ahmed Lutfi Efendi, although some Christian monuments were removed, the Sultan ordered the preservation of the angels' faces, some of which can still be seen today. Renamed Aya Sofia by the Ottomans, this religious building is a unique record of the evolving relationship between two major religions and empires.

The Spitalfields area of East London has witnessed and provided sanctuary to those fleeing persecution. In 1743, a building on Fournier Street was erected as a Huguenot temple. It would then be converted into a Wesleyan chapel, a Methodist Church, the Spitalfields Great Synagogue and, in the 1970s, a mosque. An original sundial with the Latin motto "Umbra Sumus" (we are shadows) remains.

In recent years religion and art have clashed, and this has ignited debates over freedom of expression and the right to protect the beliefs of minority groups. This is not a new phenomenon and religious leaders such as the Prophet Muhammad (pbuh) have been satirized or vilified for centuries depending on the current war, land occupation or trade dispute. An excellent article by the journalist Mehdi Hasan points out that the Prophet Muhammed survived Dante's inferno in the Divine Comedy.[5] It's a pretty gruesome description and makes most poor-quality Youtube films that attack Islam appear pretty tame.[6]

The Prophet Muhammad (pbuh) understood how the arts could be used to change opinion. According to Dr Usama Hasan, an Islamic scholar and scientist, 7th-century Arabian culture was dominated by an oral tradition, and poetry was used for propaganda and psychological warfare, being employed effectively by the Prophet Muhammad (pbuh), with Hassan bin Thabit and Abdullah bin Rawaha amongst his most skillful composers of verse. "Your verses hurt them far more than our arrows," the Prophet observed to Hassan.[7]

---

[5] Medhi Hasan, "Muhammad survived Dante's Inferno. He'll Survive a YouTube Clip," in *The Huffington Post*, 02/10/12.

[6] Dante Alighieri (1995) *The Divine Comedy*. New York: Everyman's Library.

[7] Usama Hasan, "No compulsion in religion: An Islamic case against blasphemy laws," A Quilliam Concept Paper, accessed February 2013, http://www.quilliamfoundation.org/wp/wp-content/uploads/publications/free/no-compulsion-in-religion.pdf.

Perhaps Caravaggio has something to teach us. He may not have been leading the "good life" but he was producing art that suddenly gave the story of Christianity a shot of adrenalin. He would allude to old masters such as Michelangelo but bring these stories into the present with extraordinary verve.

The endlessly evolving DNA of our public imagination needs to be fed by the images and stories of the past and the present and this is above all an open invitation. Our communal imagination contains timeless messages to be used and reused, not to be shelved in a dusty corner of our collective memory.

Historically, religion and the imaginative arts have a heavy presence in this global and timeless archive and we all have a right to access this rich collection. It will lead to a more profound understanding of the world.

As the poet Seamus Heaney writes in his collection of essays entitled, *The Government of the Tongue*:

> In its repose the poem gives us a premonition of harmonies desired and not inexpensively achieved. In this way, the order of art becomes an achievement intimating a possible order beyond itself, although its relation to that further order remains promissory rather than obligatory. Art is not an inferior reflection of some ordained heavenly system but a rehearsal of it in earthly terms; art does not trace the given map of a better reality but improvises an inspired sketch of it.[8]

---

[8] Seamus Heaney (1990) *The Government of the Tongue: Selected Prose, 1978-1987*. New York: Farrar, Straus and Giroux.

Forged in the Fires of Belief: An Exploration of Faith and Volunteering in Attend

David Wood

Our journey: faith and volunteering intertwine

I grew up in a world where I don't remember ever hearing the term "volunteering." In fact, I don't recall the concept coming into my consciousness until I was nearly thirty and became a director of an adult hospice.

So did I grow up in a self-obsessed, materialistic Britain? Not in the least. It was a household whose whole fabric was enmeshed in the local church. Almost every evening one or the other of us was at the church, be it in a leadership or supporting capacity. At the weekends, Saturdays were spent at the church tennis club, and Sundays in services or at youth events. Even our annual family holidays were spent organising church holidays. So was this volunteering? It didn't feel like it, it was just a way of life, and as a child I did not even realise it wasn't what everyone else was doing.

Interestingly, our activities did not extend much beyond the faith community. Engagement with the wider world was essentially through low-key evangelistic activity. We certainly didn't engage with what I have come to now understand as the wider voluntary sector.

Encountering the League of Friends

Just over ten years ago, I became the Chief Executive of the National Association of Hospital and Community Friends (which became Attend in 2006). I was aware of the activities of local Friends Groups, having encountered their work while my wife was a ward sister in a local NHS hospital. My expectation was that I had become involved in the leadership of a totally secular organisation: one whose inspiration came from a shared vision to meet a need in the local community, and that caused people to band together in a common mission.

Almost immediately that perception was challenged. Within the first three months I attended regional conferences throughout the UK. Universally, they were opened with a thought for the day, which was led by a hospital chaplain or a local cleric. One weekend event even had a full church service, which was an integral part of the programme.

Exploring the early roots of the organisation

So in those early days I realised there were things I didn't understand about the history of the League of Friends, and that to be Chief Executive I would need to try and work out what it was all about, and what the organisation's core values were.

Like many such movements there are tales of particular local projects, documented not least because they inspire a community, and the audience for these stories is clear. However, the history of all but the most successful of national bodies tends to be hazier. In a bookcase, I discovered a book I had inherited from my predecessor, written by Dame Lesley Whateley, who had been commissioned by Lady Moncton and Lady Macleod: great names in the history of the movement.

In her history, Dame Leslie supports the idea that the movement can justly claim to descend from the middle of the eighteenth century, and highlights its religious roots. Hospitals and infirmaries date from medieval times; their provision was an obligation of Church and was most often delivered by monastic orders. After the medieval times, thinking came more into line with models we would recognise today. Religious leaders such as Bishop Maddox of 1746, to whom the Infirmary at Worcester owes its inception, were great advocates of the hospital movement and were very influential in its development.[1]

Even in 1949, when the national body was founded, there was a strong humanitarian spirit which challenged the professional correctness. Challenging the rather correct objectives to "...mobilise, encourage, foster and maintain the interest of the public in the patients and the

---

[1] Leslie Whateley (1974) *Yesterday, Today and Tomorrow: History of the National Association of Hospital Friends*. Law and Local Government Publications.

support of the work of hospitals in Great Britain," Captain J. W. Price proposed that they should read:

> To mobilise, encourage, foster and maintain, the human love of the people of this Country, in the giving of service to supplement the healing work of the staff and the State, and always ensure a humanising supplement to the work of the hospitals.[2]

While these changes were not adopted they make it clear that there is far more to the organisation than what it does: it is about values, and the very nature of who we are.

Bringing it up to date

Clearly, faith service and obligation were entwined together in the very roots of the organisation. There was clearly also some practical expression of faith in the organisation ten years ago, but evidence of this was fading.

I was forced to ask myself a number of questions:

1. Was this merely a social religious practice which was congruent with the value set of the community of activity, essentially a reflection of middle-class values?

2. Was this volunteering activity a practical expression of faith by people in the community?

3. Was it part of a low-key religious outreach, or just a value-driven response to a recognised need of fellow human beings?

Those thoughts had sat with me for ten years, and, until now, had never been explored. However, I recently conducted a series of ten interviews with a diverse range of individuals from our local member organisations. This paper presents three of these interviews as a starting point for an analysis of our volunteers' motivations.

---

[2] The National Association of Leagues of Hospital Friends, Executive Minutes of 5th May 1949.

Exploring the motivations of members from local groups

The organisation is much like a large family: trust is based on a quality of relationship, and that develops over time. Having been in post for over ten years, I have been privileged to have lots of conversations with many different people: conversations that tend to stray, conversations which show what people value, and what they believe. I didn't necessarily know that I was speaking to people of personal faith, I just had a hunch.

So, in thinking about interviewing some of these people, it was relatively easy to draw up a long list of twenty or so whom I might speak to. In picking my sample, I was keen to ensure the following:

- A geographical spread: that there are interviewees from England, Wales and Scotland.

- A mix of younger and older people, of men and women.

- Individuals who volunteered with organisations who had a clear faith-based mission, and those who did not.

- People who came from different backgrounds, and were likely to have different life experiences.

Initially, I was thinking of faith in the broadest of senses, but in my reflections I realised that our membership was most likely to come from a Christian background. So, in considering the size of the sample, and the potential pitfalls of extending beyond the Christian faith, I decided to focus on this one area.

Having created a shortlist of ten interviewees, ensuring I had the diversity I wanted, I wrote to them. All those contacted agreed to be interviewed.

The approach I adopted was to conduct a planned telephone interview, which varied in length but lasted at least an hour.

The discussions focused on three areas:

1. How their lives and values had been shaped, and particularly how that had been intertwined with the church.

2. How volunteering had become part of their lives, and how it had expressed itself practically.

3. The interviewees' perception of why they did what they did, and how much it is rooted in religious beliefs.

Underpinning the questions were a number of hypotheses I was seeking to test, namely:

Role of volunteering

- That volunteering would be evidenced both within the church as well as in the wider community.

Sense of vision and values

- That there would be a considered coherence around vision and values and how they are applied on a daily basis.

The influence of faith

- That the volunteers would clearly identify their community activity as a response to their faith.

From those ten volunteers initially interviewed, three diverse examples have been selected for inclusion in this chapter. Initially, I present the information gathered in a biographical format.

Joe Hyland
SOS Bus Northern Ireland
Year of Birth: 1955

Early foundations
Joe's memories of his early life reveal a tough existence. His father was a construction engineer travelling the world, while his mother was left in Manchester to work and bring up the three children. During his early teens, Joe describes little engagement with his parents, and essentially he was brought up by his grandparents. It was a family in which there were strong values, but they weren't voiced. There was no rhetoric around the rights and wrongs in life.

Joe's mother became an alcoholic, and paid very little attention to her children or their education. He took solace in sport, and that largely became his world, becoming very accomplished in both trampolining and high diving. Aged seventeen, he joined the Armed Forces and became a Royal Engineer, just to get away from a troubled home.

Sense of values and purpose

When in his forties, and married with children, a chiropractor broke Joe's neck while he was receiving treatment. It was a time of unfathomable despair, when life had no purpose and didn't seem worth continuing. For some five years Joe had full back spasm and longed for relief or for a sense of purpose. Joe tells of how he searched for God and couldn't find him. Feeling unworthy and desperate, he and his wife, Jackie, looked over the edge of his life and considered ending it. Shortly before this could come about, however, a prayer was passionately expressed and Joe's children were given back their father, Jackie a husband and a life was given a new purpose.

Many people around Joe were supporting him on his journey into faith, something he didn't always appreciate. It was a rocky time, and he describes it "as much about wanting to leave the darkness, as to find the light to come."

As we discussed Joe's perception of the world, he highlighted that core to his understanding of God was getting the correct sense of perspective. God sees each one of us as his child; we are all a "work in progress." Many things happen in people's lives that distort, change and even crush what they were meant and intended to be. Joe views everyone from this perspective which helps him to recognise the true potential in others. This is fundamental to Joe's personal mission in life which he summarises as "to empty churches, not fill them." His personal contribution is to come alongside and help people understand how they can personally make a difference, if only they have the vision and courage to get out on the streets and unconditionally help others.

He recognises that people do not always feel equipped to volunteer. However, his experience has been that you discover what you are truly gifted to do as you try new things, and challenge yourself. It is our own perceptions of self that limits what we do, and it is that perception, the illusion of self, which we need to break down if we are truly to empower others.

Joe describes that "as faith came" his initial purpose was to heal individuals, something he saw as a tangible physical act. Over time, though, Joe's understanding of God's purpose for him has changed, matured and broadened. Today he helps to enable others through teams of people working together in the healing of communities. His aim is for us all to be an example and to bring what help we can to just one person at a time.

Service to the community

Joe clearly relishes a challenge: he is driven to make significant social change in the communities in which he works.

At Fisherwick, a Presbyterian Church in Belfast, Joe was part of the Property Committee where he oversaw a £775,000 renovation of the building. "This was a wonderful opportunity to make the church God's living room and to make the place feel special."

Joe is CEO of the charity SOS Bus Northern Ireland; his role, he says, is to create a mechanism that allows people to connect and support each other. Every Friday and Saturday, from 9pm through to 3am, the SOS Bus is in Belfast city centre supporting people as they come out of the pubs and clubs. Joe inspires over four hundred volunteers to leave their homes and go out onto the streets of Belfast to make a difference in the lives of others. Joe doesn't see his purpose as to encourage them to save souls, "That's the Holy Spirit's job." Instead, he wants to envision a "dancing in the streets," offering positive role models, showing unconditional love, and expecting nothing in return. Joe believes that in being selfless we inspire a response from others which brings about genuine change in our communities. Already, the Belfast police service has noticed a reduction in violent crimes.

Reflecting

"It's easy to be a rebel, to kick hard against people and systems we can't control. However, our fundamental purpose is to help transform the world just one person at a time. Transformation is not about judgement. It doesn't involve inflicting hurt and pain – though change is always tough, even when for the better – it's about lovingly supporting people and communities to be what God knows they were intended to be."

Website
www.sosbusni.com

Kath Fox MBE
Deeside Community Hospital League of Friends
Year of Birth: 1931

Early foundations

Kath was born in a small mining village in North Wales. She was the eldest of six children, and so responsibility came at an early age. It was a very different world to the one we live in today, essentially much harder. One example Kath gave was her memory of the first ever paid holiday miners had in 1938. Another was when her Father was called up at the beginning of the war; she can remember walking up to the pit with him to collect his pick and shovel, as you had to buy your own tools. As she reiterated, not an expectation people would have today!

Chapel was a big part of Kath's childhood: it gave life a sense of pattern. Every Sunday her family went to Chapel three times: morning, afternoon Sunday school and evening. An example of the importance of Sunday school was the annual outing, the only holiday that young Kath had. Every year, without fail, six coaches of young people would travel for a day out to Rhyll. It was a day of excitement, and forms one of her enduring memories of childhood.

Kath won a scholarship to the Grammar School in Wrexham. It had a strong religious ethos that Kath appreciated. She was marked for leadership at a young age, being appointed a prefect a year earlier than usual.

Service to the community

With a large family, Kath was used to helping at home, but was also encouraged to help in the wider community. She remembers frequently going visiting with her Mother. During her childhood Kath had both scarlet fever and diphtheria, both of which meant six weeks in isolation hospitals. During the epidemics lots of her friends died. This gave her an enduring sense of the fragility of life.

When it came to a career, Kath was undecided whether to go into nursing or teaching. To help her decide, her mother arranged for her to go voluntarily to the local hospital. All ended happily when she began training at Alder Hey in January 1948. During her training, Kath only got one day off a week which made regular church attendance difficult.

Next she worked in Chester. When she married, she was a sister in an isolation hospital. Her next role was to train for midwifery. Working in the tenements in Liverpool, Kath found a whole new understanding of both poverty and need. She recalls going to do home deliveries, and the only running water was one tap on a landing for three families. Also, once the new delivery had arrived, very few had cots, and the baby's first resting place was a drawer.

During midwifery, Kath came across lots of foetal abnormality caused by various diseases and other issues such as thalidomide. At that time, little was known before the birth, and it was often the midwife who was the first to challenge her view of the world, dealing with the shock, pain and confusion that accompanied issues which we might not consider life threatening today. Also, the extreme poverty meant babies often died of gastroenteritis. Even when babies got well, sometimes families just didn't collect them. Kath says it tested everything about her: it made her question her faith, and also strengthened it.

Finally, Kath was appointed matron of a community hospital. In a position of such significant leadership, where people looked to her for answers, Kath often found herself relying on her faith more and more.

Involvement in volunteering

Kath only got involved with Friends when she retired from Deeside Hospital in 1997, and she came straight in as Chairman of the group. Friends of Deeside Hospital seeks to raise funds for the hospital and its patients, as well as providing a chaplain. She comments that the role can be as challenging as some of the paid ones she has previously taken on, as she seeks to provide a level of comfort that Deeside Hospital would not be able to offer otherwise.

She also does a lot for the cancer network, talking to GPs and radiographers during their training on how to deliver bad news.

Sense of values purpose

As the story of Kath's life and career unfolded, it was evident that she has devoted her life to people and supporting them.

Kath indicated that she had a really good marriage, for over fifty two years. Without the support and encouragement of her husband, who shared her Christian principles and greatly valued the importance of the family and the extended family, her life would have been very different.

She has twin sons, two great daughters-in-law and five grandchildren who give her so much love and care, especially since her husband died. She believes she is a very fortunate person.

Reflecting
Kath says the basis for all of her life was the pattern set in her childhood. At a young age that pattern was about church and community being intertwined. Throughout her story there is a real thread of being personally challenged by poverty and disadvantage, and offering something of herself to help people overcome that.

Janet Mountain
Space 109
Year of birth: 1948

Early foundations
Janet was born in Hillingdon, and grew up in Hayes in Middlesex. Her father ran the family business, a grocer's. Janet recalls that both she and her sister were expected to help in the shop from a young age.

Janet enjoyed school, and wanted to be an important part of things. She was particularly pleased to be made a prefect.

Her initial aspirations were to work in childcare, but her home environment didn't support that. Her first job was in a boarding school. Janet has had a number of roles in her career, all of which are about people and the wider community.
Janet's grandparents were strong Methodists, and she enjoyed going to Sunday school when she visited them in Scarborough.

Involvement in volunteering
Janet didn't really get involved in volunteering until she was sixteen. A colleague at work asked her to help out with cub scouts, and it became a real interest for about ten years. She enjoyed everything from learning and teaching the badges, to going to the camps and jubilees.

Janet gave this up when the family came along. After some happy times, Janet found herself on her own and with a small child, looking for answers. When taking the cub scouts away, she had been particularly impressed by the verger of the church where they had stayed, and set out to find him. As she walked through the graveyard to the church, the first thing she came across was his headstone, and it felt devastating. Janet took her small son back into the town for lunch.

As she was about to leave the café, a women pressed a piece of paper into her hand which said "Jesus saves" and her journey to faith had begun. The journey was completed during a time when Janet was unwell with a slipped disc in 1982.

Janet then describes how her career and her Christian and community contributions developed in parallel. An example would be that as part of her career she became a trainer and gained her teaching certificates and assessor skills. She was then able to utilise these skills in her work within the voluntary sector.

Another example was that she became heavily involved in project management for York Hospital, the largest project being the remodelling of the front entrance area. She was then to use those skills with York Hospital League of Friends.

Janet has also been trained in management and leadership, and supplemented this with a theological course. This meant that her skills have been recognised in a number of ways, including through being made a house group leader and a Chairman of Deacons. Janet is also a Director of Horizon Ministries which focuses particularly on supporting women to grow in their faith. Janet's role is a development one, running days which enable people to reflect. She specifically sees this as supporting the role of the local church.

A sense of values and purpose

Janet's recounting of her involvement in Space 109 highlighted her approach. Begun in 2006, Space 109 is a home-grown charity providing community arts activities and events in Walmgate in York and the city beyond. Its aim is to strengthen and unite the community through self-expression; it involves 5000 people across its spectrum of activities, which cater for all ages.

Janet had a particular burden for the area of York where Space 109 is now based, many years before it was ever conceived. Not long after the project had been established, she saw an advert looking for help to write a business plan, but it just wasn't the right time for her to help. Then Janet was helping Attend with a regional event, and met the founder. Within months she had been invited to be a trustee, and soon took the role of Chair. Repeatedly, her life has had a symmetry where things have come together: her skills, beliefs and interests.

Reflecting

Janet reflects that from an early age she recognised the need to achieve, and this has driven her to succeed.

Her strongest sense is that she needs to achieve, to be the best that she can be so that she can change society for the better. Better, for Janet, is holistic, it can be within the church, or the wider community. She says her life is a living testament to the fact that the two are intertwined, and it can be both.

Website

www.space109.org

Applying a theoretical framework

When conducting the interviews, the diversity of the stories was striking, and this diversity is reflected in the three examples selected here. To bring them together, the following framework helps us to consider an individual's motivations to engage in voluntary action. It brings together two well-established motivational theories that have been developed from different perspectives: a traditional needs-based model[3] and one which assesses donor motivations.[4]

Understanding the elements of the models

1.   A needs-based model of motivation:

---

[3] David McClelland (1961) *The Achieving Society*. New Jersey: D Van Nostrand.
[4] Russ Prince and Karen File (1994) *The Seven Faces of Philanthropy: A New Approach to Cultivating Major Donors*. New Jersey: Jossey-Bass.

McClelland's theory (1961) describes three types of motivational need.

1. *Achievers*: the need for achievement. "Achievers" seek to attain realistic but challenging goals, and advancement in their role or situation. There is a strong need for feedback as to achievement and progress, and a need for a sense of accomplishment.

2. *Influencers*: the need for authority and power. "Influencers" seek to be effective and to make an impact. There is a strong need to lead and for their ideas to prevail. There is also motivation and a need towards increasing personal status and prestige.

3. *Affiliators*: the need for affiliation. "Affiliators" have a need for friendly relationships and are motivated towards interaction with other people. The affiliation driver produces motivation and need to be liked and held in popular regard. These people are team players.

2. The seven faces of philanthropy:

The work of Prince and File (1994) considered why people give to charity. They identified seven key reasons, which are outlined below:

- The *Communitarian*: Giving Makes Sense

- The *Devout*: Giving is God's Will

- The *Investor*: Giving is Good Business

- The *Socialite*: Giving is Fun

- The *Altruist*: Giving Feels Right

- The *Repayer*: Giving in Return

- The *Dynast*: Giving is a Family Tradition

Typical characteristics of each "face" are outlined in appendix 1.

Looking at the model in the context of the interviews

The application of these models is not an exact science, and there are several limitations to consider. For example, "The Seven Faces" model was developed in order to think about donor motivations, and there is a difference between the kinds of motivations involved in donating money and those associated with volunteering. In addition, a single interview naturally has drawbacks when it comes to accurately gauging people's motivations.

As a stimulus for discussion, however, there is value to an analysis of the volunteers in this way, and in looking through the stories and considering them against the framework, the following associations can be made.

Interviewee: Jo Hyland

Source of motivation	Reference
"Achiever"	Committed to projects with tangible outcomes (for example: renovation of building to create a positive environment).
"Influencer"	Seeks to inspire others to work together in healing communities.
The *Communitarian*: giving makes sense	Sees the extent of life within the community as a measure of personal success.
The *Devout*: giving is God's will	Own volunteering is motivated by a sense of personal purpose and mission.
The *Altruist*: giving feels right	Fundamental purpose is to help to transform the world – one person at a time.

Interviewee: Kath Fox

Source of motivation	Reference
"Influencer"	Supports GPs and radiographers in their training on how to deliver bad news, and is committed to helping people overcome poverty and disadvantage.
The *Devout*: giving is God's will	Being involved with supporting disadvantaged people strengthened her faith.
The *Altruist*: giving feels right	Devoted her life to people and supporting them.
The *Dynast*: giving is a family tradition	A strong family legacy that church and community life is inseparable.

Interviewee: Janet Mountain

Source of motivation	Reference
"Achiever"	Motivated to volunteer in projects, bringing professional skills to provide specialist roles.
"Influencer"	Utilises trainer and facilitator skills and experience to encourage people to develop and make a fuller contribution themselves.
The *Devout*: giving is God's will	Strong belief that volunteering is a living testament to the fact that faith and work within the community can be intertwined.
The *Altruist*: giving feels right	Keen to optimise her personal capacity and contribution to change society for the better.

Drawing the Threads together

The interviewees told their stories; there was little prompting and they all had their own emphasis, a slightly different slant. Therefore, when we look to draw the threads together it is inevitable that we are going to see a real diversity. The above framework, demonstrated with three volunteers, was applied to all of the ten interviewees, and the results were compared. This is best summarised in a simple bar chart.

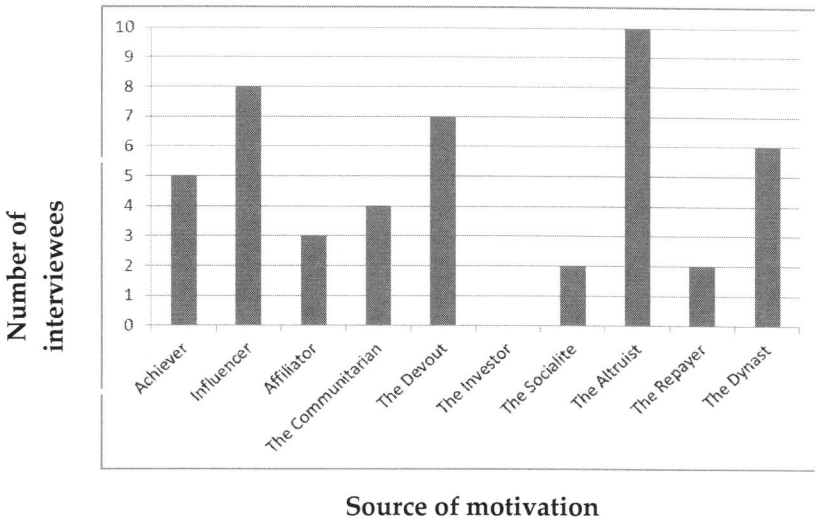

Source of motivation

Overall, interviewees' motivation seemed to identify more with a desire to influence (eight of ten) than a need to affiliate with others (three out of ten). Achieving goals was seen as important to half of the respondents. It would be said that there is a real desire to make the world a better place, and less of a need to do that with other people.

Then, drawing from the work on why people give, there was a strong common thread of altruism in all ten interviews. Faith-related values and beliefs were also important, together with family traditions.

In the light of my initial hypothesis, the sense from the interviewees varied:

- There was a definite sense that these were all activists and pragmatists: they did a lot. There were clearly differing balances on time spent in work directly linked to church, and time outside. One of the things that shone through is that in both situations the interviewees repeatedly found themselves in leadership roles.

- There seemed to be less of a considered framework behind the activity which drew from personal faith. While it was clearly there in some cases, there was also a sense that it was the interview questions themselves that prompted the reflection that joined the dots.

However, it was evident that all the interviewees threw themselves into their activities whole-heartedly. This wasn't an intellectual response, it was more about passion for their fellow man and woman, and a willingness to roll up their sleeves, get their hands dirty, and try and make the world a better place.

So can we change the World? Do these stones help us on our journey to the future?

In 2011, Frances Maude (Minister for the Cabinet Office, and Paymaster General) and Nick Hurd (Minister for Civil Society) stated: "Our ambition is to stimulate a step change in giving ... to make it easier to give time and money ... to give better support to the trailblazers and innovators."

And we have seen the thrust of that in many different ways. Following a cautious reaction to Big Society, we have seen some reflection and reassessment, but the experts haven't really come up with an answer that produces the mass engagement sought.

The Chairman of the Association of Volunteer Managers, John Ramsey, stated in 2008 that he is "not a believer in the existence of altruistic volunteering, of giving with no regards for yourself." His view is that "the volunteering relationship is not a one way altruistic pathway, but a two-way reciprocal relationship."[5] Such mantras have become embedded in the philosophies of the gurus at Number 10, and so, for example, we are seeing the proliferation of time-banking initiatives across government departments. This is not, and never will be, volunteering. It is simply a cashless exchange of goods and services.

What these simple interviews have suggested to me is that, across a range of men and women from their mid-40s to early 80s, altruism is alive and well; the three examples I have included here reflect this trend. And, where there is a "payback" for the volunteers, reflection has to be given to the concept that this payback is in the sphere of their faith. While some interviews touch on a sense of responsibility, it is much more sophisticated than that. It is not about "what we do" but who we are.

---

[5] John Ramsey (2008) "Is bad volunteer management the only refuge for altruistic volunteering?" from Association of Volunteer Managers, accessed February 2013: http://www.volunteermanagers.org.uk/bad-volunteer-management-only-refuge-altruistic-volunteering.

Could There Be Treasures in Our Faith? The Recognition and Utilisation of Spiritual Capital Values

Charles Oham

This chapter elucidates the concept of spiritual capital, a nascent concept that is paradoxically both as old as man and a currently emerging line of enquiry. This resource has been the engine of community development, innovation and resilience when appropriated by its custodians. The chapter argues for its use not just amongst people of faith but for all stakeholders, as the benefits transcend a parochial perspective. Examples of spiritual capital in practice are cited in this chapter. The chapter concludes with the benefits and challenges of spiritual capital.

First Fruit Group

In 1997, Peter Watherston, a Vicar, and his wife, Hannah, set up the social enterprise, First Fruit Trading. They started with the creation of an employment support project which addressed high unemployment and social exclusion in the London Borough of Newham. This evolved into First Fruit Group, which has been highly prolific and socially innovative in addressing unemployment and homelessness through several business initiatives.

First Fruit subsidiaries have included a sewing business that makes cheerleading outfits, coffee shops, hostels and clothes/plastic recycling. The largest is First Fruit Warehouse, which sells used office furniture collected from corporate firms. Most of the business units have an environmentally sustainable dimension to their operation; most of the furniture and white goods are snatched up just in time from the land fill.

Over the last ten years First Fruit Group has employed hundreds of people, including the vulnerable and excluded in various capacities. They have also generated a combined turnover of £10 million in trading income. Only fifteen percent of their income is attributed to grant funding.

First Fruit Group is currently navigating the current economic storm with a robust and difficult restructuring process. At times like these, most social entrepreneurs reflect on what success is to them. For Peter, success is "philosophical," it is more about the intangible than the tangible. The tangible may cease but their convictions and values will live on in the lives of those they have touched through various interventions. They have made investments in people over the years. This is their real legacy, the development of human and social capital, which is not easily measured by box ticking exercises. This kind of outlook can lead to future opportunities that may elude traditional business thinkers, as the team are not afraid to close down declining business arms and start up new ones in areas of low productivity and need. Peter and Hannah's driving force has been their faith. First Fruit was set up after Peter and Hannah left Mayflower Family Centre, an Anglican organisation in Canning Town, East London.

First Fruit Group's case goes on to demonstrate that there could be various drivers other than a social one that could propel an individual to become a social entrepreneur.

Spiritual capital

Professor Muhammad Yunnus, a Nobel Laureate and founder of the Grameen Bank, a micro credit social enterprise which has lent over seven billion dollars to the poor in Bangladesh, challenges the idea that it is a one-dimensional human being who plays the role of an entrepreneur. Mohammad comments that "we insulate the person from other dimensions of life; such as religious, emotional and the political."[1] These dimensions can in fact have a great impact on the motivations for entrepreneurialism.

One driver of social entrepreneurship, for example, is religious in nature, and is known as spiritual capital; it is quite nascent as a research line

---

[1] Muhammad Yunnus, "Social Business Entrepreneurs are the Solution," in Alex Nicholls, ed. (2006) *Social Entrepreneurship New Models for Social Change*. Oxford: Oxford University Press.

compared to the other forms of capital postulated by Pierre.[2] Yale Research Professor, Theodore Malloch, describes spiritual capital as the advantages a person derives from their faith which manifests in their values and is experienced in their relationships and commitments amongst people. He notes that spiritual capital provides a link to a transcendental form of "refined" happiness, going on to posit that it is "founded on an understanding that all resources are entrusted to people."[3] This therefore demands stewardship through the preservation and development of a wealth of resources. Spiritual capital can be described as "wealth we can live by drawing upon our deepest meanings, values and highest motivations, it helps make the future of humanity sustainable."[4]

On a strategic level, spiritual capital can add value to Government-led initiatives like Big Society and, more recently, the Prime Minister's call for the British to be proud of their Christian heritage and the creation of "moral markets" that would stem unethical corporate culture driven by short term gain. The Leader of the Opposition, Ed Miliband, also advocates a longer-term approach to business performance evaluation and a curb to the bonus culture in the City.

A major challenge spiritually-driven social entrepreneurs may face in a secular society is societal perceptions about the role and limits of faith. However, judging by our poor performance as a nation in addressing societal dilemmas such as inequality and youth unemployment and their effects on society, one would wonder why a rethink is not necessary.

Nevertheless, most social entrepreneurs are resolute. Lord Mawson, who founded the famous Bromley by Bow Centre as a church leader, became a social entrepreneur by working in Britain's poorest estates by committing to applying business principles to social issues.[5] Currently, Bromley by Bow Centre – situated in one of the most deprived boroughs in the United Kingdom, Tower Hamlets – has birthed over 28 social enterprises and employs over two hundred people.

[2] Richard Jenkins (2002) *Pierre Bourdieu*. Oxford: Routledge, p. 85.
[3] Theodore Roosevelt Malloch, "Spirituality and Entrepreneurship," in Nicholas Capaldi, ed. (2006) *Business and Religion A Clash of Civilizations?* Salem, MA: M&M Scrivener Press.
[4] Danah Zohar and Ian Marshall (2004) *Spiritual Capital: Wealth We Can Live By*. San Francisco: Berrett-Koehler.
[5] Andrew Mawson (2008) *The Social Entrepreneur: Making Communities Work*. London: Atlantic Books.

Social enterprise: a holistic approach to capital

A key strength of social entrepreneurs is a holistic reliance on all forms of capital to achieve their objectives. A social entrepreneur manages these inputs to create a socially innovative and relevant output that generates social value. Some forms of capital that are exploited to the maximum are human, social, cultural, economic and spiritual capital. Determined social entrepreneurs can initiate thriving projects without economic capital, demonstrating the fluidity of the forms of capitals. Unlike others, these entrepreneurs believe before they see, and in entrepreneurship theory values like this can be evaluated as a superior form of opportunity recognition, thus revealing the benefits social entrepreneurs contribute to society.

The term "social enterprise" could be restrictive, depending on how the word "social" is applied. However, it is a loose and all-encompassing term for all formations of trading activity within the third sector. The term can conceal the fact that there could be more than one reason, other than a social objective, for which these organisations are set up. Although the outcomes are usually social, the term "social entrepreneur" ought to be used loosely for a range of objectives, which may include the social, spiritual, philosophical and so on. Stakeholders have been able to understand the practice of social entrepreneurship but have failed to grasp a broader perspective; the reasons why people trade for an altruistic purpose.

This point is critical due to the scale and enormity of the challenges facing mankind today, which includes low food security, increasing poverty levels and divides, unsustainable environmental practices and use of finite resources. Loosely defining the term "social enterprise" will enable stakeholders to understand and engage with this phenomenon and to access a wider range of benefits that can accrue from a spectrum of motivations which compel social entrepreneurs to do what they do.

Spiritual capital as a social objective

One may ask, what do these organisations have in common: Islamic Relief, Green Pastures, Jewish Care, PECAN, Nishkam Civic Association, Bromley by Bow Centre, LifeLine Projects, Street Pastors, and Christians Against Poverty? Their *raisons d'être* are their spiritual convictions which manifest as a social objective. A 2007 NCVO review of public policy outlined a number of reasons why governments are keen to engage with faith communities, they included: faith-based communities acting as a repository and transmitter of social values, a focal point for ethnic minority communities, command and contribution of resources and community cohesion and integration.

In addition to this, funding from the Government is becoming less cumbersome. In a 2008 survey by the Communities Development Foundation, a third of faith-based organisations surveyed managed to access funding from local or regional government. The Government in recent years has taken proactive steps to mitigate against funding bias. In March 2010, for example, the Communities and Local Government Department introduced a document entitled "ensuring a level playing field..." to demystify some myths and stereotypes stakeholders held about public funding of faith-based organisations.

Benefits of spiritual capital

Spiritual capital offers a number of benefits to a nation or enterprise. Firstly, it has the potential to allow for greater innovation, as the link to a "bigger source" may help us to perceive and do things differently, "thinking outside the box." Secondly, it encourages stewardship of resources, which instils the values of waste avoidance and doing more with little, principles which strike a chord in these times. Stewardship modelling may in fact be the answer to the challenges being faced by the NHS and the Public Sector.

A third benefit is the availability of human resource; that religious centres can serve as human resource repositories is heartening for community development. A fourth benefit is the potential for partnership and collaborations which increases the outputs and outcomes as a result of the leveraging and scaling up of resources, as well as the critical mass of competitive advantage each partner brings to the table.

A good example is the Joint Churches Aid that provided humanitarian relief in an effective and coordinated manner in the former Republic of Biafra between 1967 and 1970. Africa Files and the Peat Report revealed that the faith-based NGOs were less bureaucratic and pragmatic, managing a network of over 2000 feeding centres in the country and effectively flying 5314 extremely dangerous missions that delivered well over 60,000 tons of food, saving millions of lives in Biafra. Morris Davis and other commentators noted that there was extraordinary inter-agency cooperation among these faith-based NGOs, both within and outside Biafra compared to their counterparts such as the Red Cross (ICRC).[6]

The fifth benefit of spiritual capital is diversity, as spiritual capital celebrates human and cultural differences in all their expressions. It has the ability to unite people from different races, ethnic groupings, faiths, backgrounds and social economic classes for societal good. The sixth benefit is the ability to franchise socially innovative and relevant business models. Christians Against Poverty, Street Pastors and Food Bank's business models are currently being replicated around the United Kingdom and Europe with no financial strings attached to the franchisees, as is the case with similar business models in the private sector.

The seventh benefit is that the societal application of spiritual capital concepts could enhance economic performance. For example the United States has one of the most successful economies, and its citizens have some of the strongest religious convictions which is not a coincidence.[7]

Finally, spiritual capital can foster the discovery of latent inspirational and beneficial legacies, as there could be treasures in the history of our faiths. An excellent case is the Alliance of Religions and Conservations (ARC). ARC has discovered that by engaging with the world's 11 major religions, they are indirectly embracing 85% of the world's population (5 billion people). They will be able to significantly address the environmental challenges affecting mankind by indirectly dealing with adherents of these faiths through their organisations. ARC recently launched the Green Pilgrimage Network which aims to engage with the 100 million pilgrims who travel to pilgrimage sites each year, by encouraging their followers to adopt "greener" behaviours.

What could be the challenges of spiritual capital? Well, the proponents of this phenomenon must be open to other ideas and ways of achieving solutions to the social challenges facing mankind. They must be meek

---

[6] Morris Davis, "Audits of international relief in the Nigerian Civil War: some political perspectives," in *International Organization*, Vol. 29, No. 2, 1975, pp. 501-512.
[7] Nicholas Capaldi, "Introduction," in Capaldi, *Business and Religion*.

enough to look across the "garden" and learn from others, such as from those with "no faith" or "other faiths." After all it is all about cooperation and collaboration. As spiritual capital values and principles are entrusted to humans, it will always be susceptible to mal-administration. This could run the risk of a loss of spiritual capital value amongst stakeholders.

In conclusion, civil society and academia must consciously seek ways of being soft on the definition of social entrepreneurship but hard on the outputs and outcomes that it delivers. We must not fall to the temptation of becoming fixated on the slight differentiations that exist within the social enterprise family. We need to raise these questions more frequently: Are our activities changing more lives? How can we operate sustainably? and How socially innovative are we as social entrepreneurs? Such enquiries are of a higher importance than the vogue "social enterprise." On a broader level, adopting a spiritual capital paradigm could reveal the "treasures in our faith."

A Biblical Theology for Engaging With Society
Hugh Osgood

The theological thinking behind faith-based social action is bound to be diverse. Compassion, of course, is a theme that is held in common, and it would be easy to write a more general article with faith-based compassion as a unifying topic. Of more interest, though, are the different attitudes to society that faith groups hold.

Within some faith traditions, aspirations and imperatives unite so that there is a not only an understanding that society as a whole would benefit from being brought fully within its particular faith framework, but an expectation that such an outcome should be every believer's goal. Of course, there need be nothing sinister about this. Indeed, it could be argued that a faith that believes it has found life's meaning yet seeks to withhold that meaning from society at large is elitist. Often, though, faith attitudes are far more complex than those who argue from such stereotypes suppose, and it is the complexity of actual faith positioning that can stimulate our thinking.

I was recently at a conference of senior Christian leaders in the UK where attitudes to society were interestingly varied. Some believed that the church had a responsibility to transform society, whilst others believed that the temporary nature of society deprioritised that responsibility, and that the church needed to think more about preparing for a society yet to be formed. It was an interesting debate and it led me to some biblical reflections which I share here to stimulate discussion across the whole range of faith streams.

Since the Bible is a historical book that claims on-going relevance, I will set my thoughts in a context that juxtaposes past and present.

The general case for Christian engagement

It had been a frantic few days. In an outpost of the Roman Empire, one that Rome had already marked down as a trouble-spot, the Roman governor was being faced with a teacher and wonder-worker whom local religious leaders had accused of claiming to be some kind of king. As Jesus stood before Pontius Pilate He eventually responded to Pilate's cross-examination. His answer was simple: "My kingdom is not of this world."[1]

So where does such an answer leave us two thousand years later? Should Christians be keen to promote community action and take on key roles in society? In this chapter we turn to the Bible for a solution and in doing so find a clear theology of intentional engagement.

From cover to cover God makes sure His instructions for living are backed up by stories of His involvement in people's lives. Some of the stories are about individuals and some about groups. In the Old Testament the group stories focus on the interplay between nations. In the New Testament they concern the church and the wider world.

Wherever we look in the Bible it is clear that God expects His people to help others as a way of showing the benefits of living in relationship with Him. And He leaves us in no doubt that the "others" we are to help must go beyond those who share our faith. We are to be helpful in the workplace, no matter who our employer happens to be.[2] We are to show love in our families and to respect rightly those in authority.[3]

As we do this, it is good to hold on to the story Jesus told about the Good Samaritan.[4] It is a story with an ingenious double twist. Firstly, it defines "neighbourliness" in terms of whom we receive from rather than whom we give to. Secondly, the hero turns out to be the one character in the story that listeners would never have thought of identifying with. After all, the man beaten by thieves would have felt like one of their own and the people who passed by on the other side of the road were the cream of their society. None of them would have thought to identify with the Samaritan man who provided the much-needed victim support. The

---

[1] John 18:36.

[2] Colossians 3:22.

[3] Colossians 3:18-21; Galatians 6 10; Romans 13:1.

[4] The parable can be found in Luke 10:29-37.

message of the story, then, is simple: get involved and cross the boundaries. For Jesus, the popular saying of the day, that "the Jews have no dealings with the Samaritans," was there to be countered.[5] People have to go out to others and make a difference.

In this chapter, though, we want to look beyond individual efforts and see how faith communities can serve the wider community. Of course, individual effort and group action are not mutually exclusive. All groups are made up of individuals. If the individuals that make up our faith communities are slow to understand the importance of their own day-to-day contacts, they are unlikely to enthuse over any joint community-serving activities. Encouraging individuals to engage enthusiastically at work and to interact positively with their families and communities is a good starting point.

The case for collective Christian engagement

Now, if the story of the Good Samaritan can inspire individual engagement, we need some stories that will stimulate our joint efforts. We will take two: one from the New Testament and one from the Old. The New Testament story is about the newly formed Christian church, birthed in Jerusalem around AD 32, whilst the other takes us back another six centuries.

Jeremiah

Our Old Testament story comes from around 580 BC when Jerusalem residents were transported beyond the Euphrates into exile in Babylon. As a diaspora community they would have had every reason to live detached lives. Their Jewish feet were on Babylonian soil but their Jewish hearts were elsewhere. Jerusalem was home and they had no loyalty to those who had plundered, persecuted and uprooted them. Yet into this exiled community came a letter – a letter from the prophet Jeremiah in Jerusalem. Its words were so radical that it changed their captive mind-set:

> Thus says the LORD of hosts,
> The God of Israel, to all who

---

[5] John 4:9.

were carried away captive,
whom I have caused to be
carried away from Jerusalem
to Babylon:

Build houses and dwell in them;
plant trees and eat their fruit.
take wives and beget sons and daughters;
and take wives for your sons
and give your daughters husbands,
so that they may bear sons and daughters
- that you may be increased there,
and not diminished.

And seek the peace of the city
where I have caused you to be carried away captive,
and pray to the Lord for it;
for in its peace you will have peace.[6]

To paraphrase Jeremiah's correspondence: God says come out of suspended animation, stop your short-term thinking, settle down, establish homes, plant trees, let your children marry one another, and (most amazingly of all) rethink your attitude to the city where you find yourselves; your peace and prosperity are dependent on its peace and prosperity.

These words must have come as a great shock. Theirs was a community that was determinedly transient – a community that did not want to be where it was. They wanted to go home. In Jerusalem they could build houses, plant trees and let their children marry one another. At home they could sing songs and celebrate. At home they could begin to forget the pain and indignity of captivity. No matter how bad things were in Jerusalem (and all the reports indicated that things were utterly desolate), it was home, and home was where they were meant to be. Rebuilding their lives in Jerusalem made more sense than rebuilding their lives in Babylon. Surely they needed to teach the Babylonians a lesson. This was no time to give the appearance of caving in and settling down by making themselves comfortable beyond the Euphrates and contributing to Babylonian society. The only society that really concerned them was Jerusalem's, and that was 500 miles away.

---

[6] Jeremiah 29:4-7 (NKJV).

Yet Jeremiah's words could not be ignored. Evidently God's perspective was not their perspective. Isolationism might be preferred but engagement was expected.

The early church

Moving on to the first century AD, we are once again in a world of correspondence. One hundred and twenty people who had seen Jesus after His resurrection took His promise of spiritual empowerment seriously and waited in an "upper" room. Once the empowerment came they spilled out onto the streets and preached to a vast crowd. Until then the listeners had known little of the divine purpose in Jesus' death and had only heard rumours of His resurrection. Now they were told that the power of His life was available to all who would come to God in repentance and faith. Within a few hours everything on the streets had changed and a church of three thousand plus was coming to terms with sins forgiven and the vibrancy of a new-found faith. Those who were baptised that day all had a sense of relationship with the living Christ and were eager to put into practice all He had taught.

In the days that followed, those who had been closest to Jesus prior to His crucifixion had their hands full, passing on all that they had heard Him say. Teaching sessions were interspersed with prayer meetings, special meals of remembrance and times of celebration and friendship. Eventually, though, persecution scattered this ever-growing band, and this is when the correspondence began.

There were letters to scattered believers and letters to new believers too. As believers dispersed from Jerusalem, Gentiles as well as Jews warmed to their life stories and responded to their bold preaching on the need for repentance towards God and faith in His risen Son. This new faith was not just a national religion, this was a faith available to all. God's plan for the nations was becoming increasingly clear. Within a few years churches were established all around the Mediterranean area and letters were penned to strengthen and encourage these worshipping communities.

However, they were more than worshipping communities. Yes, they definitely looked inwards and upwards, yet they looked outwards too. Their lives had been changed by the events of the cross and they had taken hold of Jesus' words, "My kingdom is not of this world."

However, they saw themselves as part of a spiritual kingdom in the midst of the world's kingdoms. Like the Jews in Babylon six centuries earlier they were a community within a community; there to be engaged, not there to stand apart. When Peter wrote to the Jewish believers who had been dispersed he said:

> Dear friends, your real home is not here on earth. You are strangers here. I ask you to keep away from all the sinful desires of the flesh. These things fight to get hold of your soul. When you are around people who do not know God, be careful how you act. Even if they talk against you as wrong-doers, in the end they will give thanks to God for your good works when Christ comes again.[7]

There are echoes here of Jeremiah's letter from six centuries earlier but Peter went further. In essence Peter was saying: "Don't stop doing good to people just because they are being negative about you. It's inevitable that society will eventually recognise the benefit of your good works, just as it's inevitable that you'll keep on doing them." It is as if Peter saw the growth of the church as directly linked to both words and works. Jesus preached, so the church had to preach. Jesus performed good works, so the church had to perform good works. The other kingdom emphasis was there but it was not the whole story. Peter knew that, in answering Pilate, Jesus had gone on to explain "If my kingdom were of this world, My servants would fight."[8] Jesus was not only confirming the present reality of His kingdom but affirming that it could stand (and grow) without recourse to the sword. His three years of preaching prior to His death and resurrection had proved this. Words and works were, and are, the way of His kingdom.

This thought of the inevitability of good works lies at the heart of the Christian gospel. Whilst it is clear that good works cannot bring us into a relationship with God or guarantee our destiny in His eternal kingdom, the relationship with God, which repentance and faith secures, leads to a change of lifestyle evidenced by good works. Paul wrote to the Ephesian church:

> For by grace you have been saved through faith, and that not of yourselves; it is the gift of God, not of works, lest anyone should boast. For we are His

---

[7] 1 Peter 2:11 (New Life Version).
[8] John 18:36.

workmanship, created in Christ Jesus for good works, which God prepared beforehand that we should walk in them.[9]

For Paul, the change that we undergo when we repent and believe in Christ is so radical that he refers to it as a new creation. Suddenly this begins to make sense of the "new kingdom" teaching that Jesus brought. We are to be new creations in a new kingdom, living in this world in such a way that it leaves everyone hoping for the day when the new kingdom will replace this world's kingdoms as the everlasting reality. Of course, the principles of entry into the new kingdom will not change and as God sees the problems in society, His ultimate plan for total transformation involves a new kingdom to be populated by people who are being transformed here and now. However, that "here and now" highlights God's current transformation programme where people who have been changed through repentance and faith bring the benefits of that change to society. Society knows that good works are essential in a world of need. Christians are empowered to meet this world's needs through the transforming work of Christ's death and resurrection and through the gift of the Holy Spirit. The church has to engage in society.

How did the early church engage?

So let's return to Jerusalem in the days before the scattering. What of those early Christians gathering in the temple court and meeting in local homes? What teaching did they hear and how was it put into practice in the Jerusalem streets?

There is no doubt that the disciples who had been closest to Jesus would have repeated all they recalled. They had been with Him when He had talked about salt and light, baskets and cities:

> You are the salt of the earth; but if the salt loses its flavour, how shall it be seasoned? It is then good for nothing but to be thrown out and trampled underfoot by men. You are the light of the world. A city set on a hill cannot be hidden. Nor do they light a lamp and put it under a basket, but on a lampstand, and it gives light to all who are in the house. Let your light so shine before men, that they may see your good works and glorify your Father in heaven.[10]

---

[9] Ephesians 2:8-10 (NKJV).
[10] Matthew 5:13-14 (NKJV).

Every listener would have known that they were to make a difference in the world around them. Thinking through the often repeated words of Jesus and reflecting on the numerous accounts of His actions, they would have known that God had turned their darkness to light and purposefully set them up for all to see. Of course, it was possible for them to hide their light but to do so would be a denial of their transformed nature. The changes happening in their lives were supposed to mark them out and achieve positive change around them.

1st Century Jerusalem was not a big city by today's standards, yet as Jesus had been proclaimed as the crucified Christ and risen Saviour thousands had come to faith. One of the reasons for this growth was that the church was birthed at the annual week-long Pentecost feast when many had travelled from other nations to be in Jerusalem. The new believers formed strong bonds with one another, as those who lived locally embraced those who, having travelled, had taken the bold decision to stay on and become established in their new-found faith. These one-time visitors needed to be housed and fed. As the newly formed church rose to the challenge, local believers shared their homes and those who had gathered from near and far did all they could to release their funds and provisions. Obviously other city residents, well aware of the influx, came to know of the sacrificial responses. It was clear that there was a new community in the midst of their already hospitable city that was pushing every boundary of generosity.

But crowds make city authorities anxious and having so many exuberant people moving around the city week in, week out was unsettling. It was less than four years since Jesus had begun teaching in their streets and less than a year since He had been crucified. Now, the crowds of "Jesus followers" seemed as big as ever and once again there were healings on the streets. A beggar had been healed at the Beautiful Gate and sick people had been laid out in the roadways, confident of being healed as one of the group's leaders walked by. No-one in Jerusalem could say that this community within a community was too self-centred to care for the city where it was based. True, these new believers wanted everyone in Jerusalem to share their faith, and they preached with this in mind. Nonetheless, the overflow of the practical generosity, love, joy and hope that marked their own shared lives was being felt everywhere within the city walls, and even in the towns beyond.

So, did the church ever hide its light in those early days? Well, there was always a risk and some of the letters to the newly formed churches urged against withdrawing from the public eye. Paul wrote to the Philippians:

> Do all things without complaining and disputing, that you may become blameless and harmless, children of God without fault in the midst of a crooked and perverse generation, among whom you shine as lights in the world, holding fast the word of life, so that I may rejoice in the day of Christ that I have not run in vain or laboured in vain.[11]

For Paul it was vital that the church never gave up its engagement with society. He wanted the church to see its public role as a privilege rather than just a duty.

Two historical misunderstandings (domination, detachment)

Nearly 2,000 years later Paul's words can still come as a challenge. In its two millennia of history, the Christian church has passed through phases of domination over society and detachment from society. In times of domination the church has tended to think that if all is well with the church, then all is well with the world. Such thinking was evident in Europe in the centuries immediately before the Reformation and was still prevalent in the century in which the Reformation occurred. In times of detachment, however, a "strangers in a foreign land" theology comes to the fore, either through conviction or in response to marginalisation.

We have seen from our two Bible stories that it is possible to have impact without domination; to be a "community within the community," fully engaged, distinct not detached, inspirational not isolated. So in addition to the times of domination and detachment there have been amazing periods in church history where effective engagement has brought lasting changes in welfare provision, healthcare, crime reduction and education. We have quoted letters from the Bible; here is an excerpt from an anonymous letter to Diognetus, possibly dating from the second century AD. It shows that the same pattern of Christian behaviour continued beyond the pages of Scripture:

> Every foreign country is to them as their native country, and every native land as a foreign country. They marry and have children... They offer a

---

[11] Phil 2:14-16 (NKJV).

shared table, but not a shared bed… They are passing their days on earth, but are citizens of heaven. They obey the appointed laws, and go beyond the laws in their own lives. They love everyone…[12]

So how do we answer those who look back on 2,000 years of church history and see either domination or detachment as better for the church and society than the theology of engagement outlined in this chapter? Well, we must do so with care, realising that both positions stem from different understandings of the New Testament's attitude to the State. In his first letter to Timothy, Paul wrote:

> Therefore I exhort first of all that supplications and prayers, intercessions, and giving of thanks be made for all men, for kings and all who are in authority, that we may lead a quiet and peaceable life in all godliness and reverence. For this is good and acceptable in the sight of our God and Saviour, who desires all men to be saved and to come to the knowledge of the truth.[13]

This would seem to indicate that the State is something separate from the kingdom of God, yet not beyond its reach. God clearly looks for righteousness in the nations.[14] However, removing the distinction between God's kingdom and the world's kingdoms, or limiting the reach of God's kingdom, leads to very different theologies of engagement with society. Of course, it could all be largely a question of timing. No-one denies that the future is in view when the Book of Revelation states:

> The kingdoms of this world have become the kingdoms of our Lord and of His Christ, and He shall reign forever and ever.[15]

However, is this future transfer to be instant or gradual? Is it to be radical, with a new heaven and new earth, or reforming, with a renewed-earth agenda? Strong convictions can produce strong conclusions. If it is gradual, with a renewed earth in view, maybe the take-over should begin now and the church should embrace a domination programme. If not, and the earth's days are numbered, surely it would be better for the church to give up on the world and detach; after all, John's first letter says:

---

[12] Tim Dowley ed. (1996) *The History of Christianity: A Lion Handbook*. Oxford: Lion Publishing, p. 67.
[13] 1 Timothy 2:1-4 (NKJV).
[14] Matthew 25:31-46; Proverbs 14:34.
[15] Revelation 11:15 (NKJV).

Do not love the world or the things in the world. If anyone loves the world, the love of the Father is not in him. For all that is in the world – the lust of the flesh, the lust of the eyes, and the pride of life – is not of the Father but is of the world. And the world is passing away, and the lust of it; but He who does the will of God abides forever.[16]

There is a love for the world that can entice into its vices; yet there is, by contrast, a greater love for the world, which in reflecting the love of God proves that it is possible to engage with the world without becoming caught in its snares. This greater love lies at the heart of all the Bible teaches. In the words of Jesus:

For God so loved the world that He gave His only begotten Son, that whoever believes in Him should not perish but have everlasting life.[17]

How society can benefit from faith engagement

Throughout this chapter our focus has been on encouraging the church to see the biblical rightness of engaging with society. In concluding we will turn this around and highlight nine points to show how society can benefit from engaging with the church, laying to rest some possible concerns as we do so.

1. The fact that the church is a community within the community indicates that the church has considerable experience in building community and ensuring community cohesion.

2. Having spread globally, the church has developed systems for connecting the local, the regional, the national and the international. Some of this is achieved through clustering around issues of doctrinal interpretation or style, leading to a denominational structure. But beyond this, the church still has formal and informal ways of interlinking denominational groups and independent congregations through large inter-church initiatives and mutual awareness enhanced by numerous levels of contact and collaboration. The diplomatic (and academic) skills required for this are relevant in society as a whole.

---

[16] 1 John 2:15-17 (NKJV).
[17] John 3:16 (NKJV).

3.   In many communities the church is still seen as a natural point of contact by the wider community. The church with its reach into most, if not all, localities can provide society with essential channels of communication.

4.   The church is largely a gathering of volunteers and the church has skills in volunteer recruitment, retention, motivation and mobilisation.

5.   The church is committed to holding its members to high levels of integrity and compassion, enhancing the calibre of the personnel it makes available.

6.   The church has a commitment to the Bible and prayer, offering society the possibility of tapping into godly wisdom and divine intervention.

7.   The church's understanding of the relationship between engagement and evangelism is that, whilst they are not mutually exclusive, one is not intended as a veil for the other. (Here we begin to touch on possible concerns.) When Christians evangelise, the response they look for has to be personal and freely given. To use engagement in the market place as a way of forcing a spiritual response makes no sense. Nominalism, where people take the title of "Christian" without discovering its reality, is not a help to the church. Merely "Christianising" society is not a logical objective. The Bible provides a balanced theology of engagement and evangelism.

8.   The church's understanding of good works does not allow for a "holier than thou" attitude. Christians cannot, and do not, claim to have a monopoly on good works. When Christian revivals have led to an increased concern for the poor, they have also (particularly in the UK) led to a lobbying for government action to match the increased Christian provision. If there is a distinctive in Christian good works, it is set out in John 3:21, which indicates that Christian good works have to be devoid of desires for self-interest as God should be the One to receive the credit:

> But he who does the truth comes to the light, that his deeds may be clearly seen, that they have been done in God.[18]

---

[18] John 3:21 (NKJV).

9. For those who have concerns about the church and the environment, the Bible teaches that God's ultimate plan involves something better than our present society and present created order; this should inspire the church to care rather than to be dismissive. Those who love butterflies don't kill caterpillars. Caring for that which we have is a first step to being entrusted with something better.

Conclusion

There is no doubt that the Bible shows that when a person enters into a personal relationship with God through the redeeming work of Jesus Christ, it opens up "another kingdom-consciousness." However, this is not to be taken as an excuse for aloof detachment from society, or as an opportunity for domineeringly imposing values. The expectation is that a transforming relationship with God will lead to a whole-hearted and generous engagement with the surrounding society. The church is to be a community within the community that brings benefit to society at large. It must lay aside every impression of being "so heavenly minded that it is of no earthly use" and adopt a theology and philosophy that says "being here, we serve here." The love of God that reaches out to every individual has to be our personal foundation, and the basis for our theology of engagement with society.

Speed & Scale
Matt Bird

Community franchising

Are you someone who wants to make a difference? Do you want to use the resources you have to build a better world? Are you willing to work hard but also want to work smart? If so, you and I have a lot in common and I'd like to encourage you to read on...

If you walk down the high street you will pass business franchises such as Costa Coffee, McDonalds, Thortons, Boots and Thrifty. Franchising is an increasingly popular way to get going in business. Business wisdom says that two thirds of business start-ups fail however only one third of business franchisees fail. Franchising provides a "business in a box" that comes with an established brand, product, customer support, financial model and systems to make the business work. Business franchises clearly exist for commercial gain however franchising has now been adopted by the church and, because it exists for community benefit, is being described as community franchising.

Community franchising is the new name for replicating the best of what the local church does to help those people most at need in their communities. It provides a "community project in a box" and utilises many of the business approaches to replicating success at speed and scale.

Speed and scale are critical because of the major changes that are happening in our society. UK debt means that significant and ongoing public sector spending cuts are required which are directly reducing welfare provision. At the same time the social needs within our communities are increasing dramatically day by day. The welfare state as we have known it is history.

Church resurgence

It is interesting that in the 1940s the church passed ownership of its schools, hospitals and welfare organisations to the state. Over recent years it seems to me that the UK church is rediscovering its community transformation muscles which for a time had become weak and flabby through underuse. We are at a point in history where there is an opportunity for the UK church to step forward and step up, in a way that it has not done for decades, to meet the needs of those people most at need in our communities.

The Prime Minister's vision for a Big Society may have had a rough ride and been misunderstood by many, but his speech in Liverpool in July 2010 inspired me into action. It was a vision for bigger people, bigger communities and smaller government enabled by greater social action, public sector reform and community empowerment. I gathered leaders of Christian social impact organisations to consider how we could respond to the vision of Big Society and how we could deliver more local transformation at national scale. These were the beginnings of The Cinnamon Network.

Instead of coming up with an idea and asking God to bless it The Cinnamon Network decided to look at what God was already doing and join in. We noticed a pattern: local Christians in a local church were responding to a local community need by developing a local solution. As this project began delivering concrete outcomes it was then visited by church leaders and activists from other communities who were interested in replicating its success. Soon there were "how to" guides, franchise agreements and networks of practitioners to share best practice, together with professional training and support. This emergent strategy was the embryo of the UK community franchising movement.

Speed & scale

Community franchising enables the average local church to own and deliver a high quality community transformation project. This approach offers a number of compelling advantages:

- An "off the peg" community transformation project which can be adapted to fit the local context without having to "reinvent the wheel."

- An established track record of delivering success across multiple communities.

- Cost effectiveness, because the project development costs have already been paid.

- An efficiency in allowing local churches to respond at speed to the needs of the people in their local community.

- A "way of working" which honours and serves local churches without their having to raise significant costs for a central charity.

It is important to recognise that the point is not community franchising, the point is pursuing the most efficient and effective way to enable the UK church to respond at speed and scale to the increasing social needs in communities. Community franchising is simply a means to an end.

Some of the leading examples of community franchising include:

- *Food Bank* - A project that provides a minimum of three days' emergency food and support to people experiencing crisis living in the UK. It started in Salisbury and has now been replicated in over 250 locations.

- *Street Pastors* - A project that trains and mobilises volunteers to respond to anti-social behaviour. It started in Brixton and has now been replicated in over 300 locations.

- *Christians Against Poverty* (CAP) - A project that provides help, advice and debt management to people who are trapped by their finances. It originated in Bradford and has now been replicated in over 200 locations.

As one of the UK's leading supermarket chains, Tesco has over seven hundred superstores in order to achieve some level of national coverage. Food Bank, Street Pastors and CAP have between two and three hundred replications each. So even as leading examples there is still some way to go before these community franchises and others are within reach in every community to the people who need them most.

At the time of writing there are 2,038 local churches who are involved in serving their communities through a community franchise model. With approximately 40,000 local churches in the UK there are many more who could become involved. The Cinnamon Network anticipates that 10,000 local churches (25% of the UK church) could become engaged with their local communities through a community franchising model. When this is achieved the UK church will be positively impacting the lives of three million people every year through community franchising alone.

The primary macro benefit of the community franchising approach is that it enables the UK church to respond both at speed and at scale to increasing social needs in our society.

The muscles of the local church

The Cinnamon Network is passionate to see the church help those people most at need in our communities. Its strategy is to strengthen the muscles of local churches for community transformation by accelerating the speed and scale of community franchising:

- Accelerator 1: *Network Learning* – Build a learning network of CEOs and leaders of social impact charities, social enterprises and church networks who are passionate about community transformation.

- Accelerator 2: *Leadership Development* – Invest in the development of the leaders of Community Franchise organisations through executive coaching, training events and residential retreats.

- Accelerator 3: *Franchising Support* – Advise local churches who have a unique community transformation project about how to make it a "community project in a box" so that other local churches can more easily replicate it.

- Accelerator 4: *Capacity Building* – Seed fund local churches, or groups of local churches working together, to replicate a recognised community franchise project in their community and provide start-up funding for new replicable community franchise models.

- Accelerator 5: *Awareness Raising* – Promote Community Franchise projects to local church leaders and Christian activists as the most effective and efficient way to impact their communities through a one stop shop website.[1]

This work of acceleration would not be possible without the trusting partnership The Cinnamon Network enjoys with established and embryonic community franchises alike.

Social breakdown

The Cinnamon Network has identified ten areas of social breakdown that it is focused on addressing. The first five issues are adopted from the Centre For Social Justice research into the pathways to poverty, and the second five added from The Cinnamon Network's action research:

1. Family breakdown
2. Educational failure
3. Worklessness
4. Addiction
5. Debt
6. Antisocial behaviour
7. Homelessness
8. Community well-being
9. Food poverty
10. Vulnerable elderly

Whilst part of the purpose of community franchising is to avoid reinventing the wheel, there is scope for a mixed economy when it comes to models. One size doesn't fit every church. For example, when looking at antisocial behaviour as an area of social breakdown there are three community franchises on offer. Street Pastors started in Brixton with three hundred replications and a rigorous fifteen-day training programme for volunteers. Street Angels began in Halifax, with 110 replications and a learn-on-the-job approach for volunteers. Town Pastors originated in Ipswich with nine replications, the work having rapidly expanded following the murder of prostitutes in that town in

---

[1] See www.cinnamonnetwork.co.uk.

2006. Between these three networks there are now over 419 projects addressing antisocial behaviour. If there was only one model I think there would be significantly less than four hundred projects.

Voluntary organisations within the most deprived communities are resource poor and so face the challenge of sustaining community impact projects. Part of the answer may be found in social enterprise projects that provide social value, training and employment opportunities and the generation of a surplus which can be reinvested in the social purpose. Most of the community franchise models to date have a charitable funding model based on donation and grant. The Cinnamon Network is now working with a group of social entrepreneurs to develop "local-church-sized" social enterprises which, once piloted, can be replicated to national scale through the community franchising strategy.

Faith based not faith biased

Faith is becoming less of an obstacle to working in the public square and when it is a problem it is becoming easier to challenge. The main issue should be answering the question, Who are the people, anywhere and everywhere, who can roll up their sleeves and deliver outcomes for those in need?

Recently, I visited a foundation to talk about community franchising and they made the bold claim, "we do not fund faith-based projects." I think this approach is wrong, I do not think that anyone can claim that one person's motive for doing good is acceptable when another person's motive for doing good is not – people are motivated to do charity and philanthropy for many reasons. I pushed back against the claim, commenting that it was discriminatory. Regardless, the claim was also wrong. I looked at a list of the foundation's beneficiaries recorded on the wall of their office and pointed out that there were a least two dozen charities listed who were faith based. I recommended an alternative approach of working with "faith-based but not faith-biased" organisations – thankfully, they agreed.

Communities Secretary Rt Hon Eric Pickles MP recently commented at The Cinnamon Network, "In the eyes of some, being religious is seen as being 'weird.' They don't want public discussion about faith, and don't want faith to have a role in our communities. Everyone – whether religious or secular – loses out from that kind of attitude. We need to ensure that all our faith groups have every opportunity to make their mark." Recent research revealed that church volunteers are contributing seventy-two million hours every year to serving communities which, together with donations and gifts in kind, are valued at over £1 billion per annum – the Christian community is certainly making its mark through community franchising and beyond.

My dream is that the whole UK church might have the reputation the Salvation Army has for always being there for the people who need help. I believe that the opportunity to achieve this reputation is offered by the speed and scale of community franchising.

What has God put in our hands to feed the hungry?

Frequently I reflect on the story of how Jesus fed five thousand people with the five loaves and two fish offered by a small boy. As I ponder I find myself identifying with the small boy and asking myself, What has God put in my hands to feed the hungry?

At The Cinnamon Network we are often asking this question of churches and individuals: What has God put in your hands to feed the hungry? To strengthen family life? To educate children failing in education? To employ the unemployed? To provide freedom for addicts? To bring jubilee to those in debt? To bring peace in the midst of aggression? To house the homeless? To bring wholeness to people? To care for the vulnerable elderly?

We believe that, whatever we give, God has a habit of multiplying it at speed and scale.

Social Innovation and Enterprise as a Ground of the Common Good: The New Inter-Religious Frontier

Francis Davis

This chapter is about collaboration and innovation. And especially innovation to address pressing social needs. I chose this subject because while in many religious, inter-faith and multi-faith contexts the struggle for justice will be lauded as a feature of our common commitments, the nature, form and impact of such a struggle can often remain flaky; worthy, but without institutional expression. And at a time when we can no longer turn to the state as we once did social innovation becomes key, for it will provide the roots to refresh and renew our future social enterprises.

First, I will turn to what I judge to be some key challenges in the area of knowledge creation and institutional leadership for faith-based social innovation and enterprise, especially in Britain. Next, I will argue in favour of redeveloping a tradition of a common search for truth through deliberate disputation. In doing so, I will suggest that faith-based institutions may discover a more profound rootedness in emerging trends in the social sciences and management studies than some forms of theology have allowed us in changing times. With this in mind I will argue, lastly, that faith-based institutions are now at a unique juncture, with an unprecedented opportunity to launch new institutions, both to re-energise and renew a fractured public sphere.

While I have discussed the chapter with those from many communities it is not an attempt to develop an inter-religious theology and will no doubt be read as significantly shaped by my own (Roman Catholic) community, although is intended to reach well beyond its increasingly inward-looking confines. It is a common call to action where any examples given are intended to be morphed, developed, re-shaped and extended for contexts beyond those I have envisioned.[1]

Leadership, language and education

It can be dangerous for a social scientist with an interest in management and leadership to write alongside contributors who include a number of those who would reach, first, to "faith" as an "idea." For theologians of hope, social research findings can seem reductive or (with reason) to have passed into the realms of spurious "scientific" claims.[2] For religious historians, current practical questions of governance may seem trivial when benchmarked against the tides and challenges of time. For those from many other walks of life the very introduction of "management" discourse into the caring realm represents a form of treachery by risking, it could be suggested, the "commodification" of love, whose focus should be the ultimate destination of human flourishing.[3]

Others may respond with the much less nuanced allegation that high principles are delightful and desirable however funds are scarce, the external environment constantly changing and the institutional pressures enormous. Alternatively, institutional leaders – for most faith communities in Britain in the end take on legal personality – may hear such anti-managerialist complaints with a particular theological ear: they may then interpret a call for total purity by confining their institutions to clerical education or seeking out only those with whom they already agree. Add to this some local contexts in which states are weak, civil society fractured and poverty growing and there arises a recipe for conflict in the making.[4]

---

[1] Earlier versions of this chapter were tested at an international conference of Vice Chancellors at Liverpool Hope University and in dialogue with Professor Philip Booth at the IEA.

[2] Robin Gill, ed. (1998) *Theology and Sociology: A Reader*. New Jersey: Paulist Press, especially the chapter by Timothy Radcliffe OP.

[3] This was the view of Michael Holman SJ in his annual conference lecture to the Catholic Education Services in 2007. It is also present in Gerald Grace (2002) *Catholic Schools: Mission, Markets, Morality*. Oxford: Routledge.

[4] I am thinking of two-thirds world settings here but, to an extent, the argument could be applied in parts of Eastern Europe. See Francis Davis, "Ideas, Institutions and Poverty Reduction in the EU: Questions for a Theology of Governance," in *International Journal of Public Theology*, Vol. 3, No. 1, 2009.

Often, these tensions are not worked out in such explicit terms: instead, they are debated with a predilection towards "metaphor" or "imagination."[5] A lay Vice-Chancellor may delight that a secular benefactor has just given a $10 million gift to the university after three years of assiduous research and relationship building, but could find such celebration slapped down by devout board members who see the grant as "a sign."[6]

We need to pay particular attention to language, the potential for inter-disciplinary miscommunication and the need to persist in a common search for truth. "Community" is a word which is often used in religious mission statements[7] and yet it can hide an inward-looking culture and glacial governance procedure.[8] Sometimes it also acts as cover to a profound disagreement as to the nature and purpose of the institution itself. Likewise "values," which, when examined more closely, may turn out to be equal opportunities statements much thinner in philosophical intent than even the claims to a normative justice made by some secular political parties.[9]

Conceivably, terms that may have had a common meaning in cultures gone by (or in one global region) may be unravelling in the face of secularisation or the pressures of the "accountingisation" of society that (arguably) characterise the modern age.[10] Even a term such as "preaching" may be contested: one outlook on Christian life may suggest that "preaching" is only undertaken by an ordained person at the Eucharistic service while others maintain it is a task of all of the baptised as they engage in communicative activities that contribute to the rebuilding of a public sphere hollowed out by the privatisation of

---

[5] Andrew Greeley (2002) *The Catholic Imagination*. California: University of California Press.
[6] This is an example I give in the political sphere in Francis Davis, "A Political Economy of The Catholic Church," in Noel Timms and Kenneth Wilson (2001) *Authority And Governance In The Catholic Church*. London: SPCK.
[7] Of 35 interviewees in UK, 34 came from institutions where "community" was included in a mission statement but all 34 understood it differently.
[8] Arthur Levine, "Higher Education As A Mature Industry," in Philip Altbach, Patricia Gumport, Donald Johnstone, eds. (2001) *In Defence of American Higher Education*. Maryland: Johns Hopkins.
[9] See Raymond Plant, "Socialism, Markets and End States," in Julian Le Grand and Saul Estrin, eds. (1999) *Market Socialism*. Oxford: Clarendon.
[10] See Kathleen Mclaughlin, Stephen Osborne and Ewan Fairlie, eds. (2002) *New Public Management: Current Trends And Future Prospects*. Oxford: Routledge.

discourse, principles and behaviour – including the search for sanctity itself.[11] In each community there is an equivalent challenge.

Confusion over terms can mean that in practice a religious institution is identical to any other, except for some of the language it uses about itself. At the other extreme, staff teams and stakeholders can feel radically disempowered because of the enormity of the brief they have been handed.[12]

A serious approach to language is vital, then, for strategic reasons: inside the metaphors of theology and religious language may be built a tendency towards an "ought" by which we might seek to order the institution but which distracts us, no matter how unintentionally, from the "is" of the practical challenges we face and the particular local conversations we need to pursue. How are we to align "community," "vision," "inspiration," "mission," "resources" and "impact" if the words have multiple meanings?

Such deliberate reflection is particularly important in secularising settings: "spirituality," "faiths," "faith motivation," "justice" and "common good" are all terms used by religious leaders and Cabinet ministers when they meet but do these people share a vocabulary and grammar? In order to attempt to link theory, practice and delivery so that principles become not personal "beliefs" – the classical secularist close-down on the wonder of a full faith – but ways of life, rich habits of virtue, expressed through organisations as well as persons, are needed.[13]

In this environment, leading a religious social enterprise becomes a work of applied theorising – a hard-headed daily pilgrimage to authenticity between an unconditionally-marketised "social product" and an admirable (but fearful) "purity."[14] This pilgrimage is carried out in the

---

[11] The example of "preaching" arises from an interviewee. For the commercialisation of spirituality see Gordon Lynch, "Dreams of the Autonomous and Reflexive Self: The Religious Significance of Contemporary Lifestyle Media," in Basia Spalek and Alia Imtoual, eds. (2008) *Religion, Spirituality and The Social Sciences: Challenging Marginalisation*. Bristol: Policy Press.

[12] The idea of a Christian education being for preparation for death comes from a former head teacher at Ampleforth Abbey. See Anthony Howard (2006) *Basil Hume: The Monk Cardinal*. London: Headline.

[13] And this is more than "managing as if faith mattered," as my friend, Helen Alford OP, discusses in her book of that name.

[14] Interview with institution head.

context of religious communities of all kinds which can be increasingly polarised, and in societies which almost certainly are.[15]

The process of generating a common understanding for carrying out faith-based social innovation therefore needs to be grounded in an open enthusiasm for debate, involving all sides of the conversation. By this I am not suggesting a simple lurch towards "free speech" (important though that may be) but that a central feature of the formation of the resources of the institution should be encouragement of a rich disputation that opens up fresh spaces for argument.

Common meanings, common terms and a common vision are much more likely to emerge from a common life than from a fractious individualism or communitarian partisanship.[16] Faith communities need to model such a struggle towards a common culture – or community of character – to both the wider faith community and society as a whole, for, as we shall see in the next section, they are increasingly under threat.

Ironically, it is the new waves of management studies and the wider social sciences, disciplines which many people of faith have treated with suspicion, in which there are emerging patterns which might assist this process.[17]

A social enterprise that knows its place: context and analysis

Among other activities, in 2009 my colleagues and I undertook two major pieces of research: the first was for the Church of England and concentrated on the Anglican contribution to social welfare.

The second study sought to quantify the scale of the English Catholic community's work alongside asylum seekers and refugees. It was

---

[15] See Antony Archer (1986) *The Two Catholic Churches: A Study in Oppression*. Norwich: SCM, and the discussion of "kingdom versus communion Church" in Timothy Radcliffe OP (2005) *What Is The Point of Being A Christian?*. London: Continuum.

[16] I am thinking here of Christian takes on "democratic capitalism" such as Michael Novak (2001) *The Spirit of Democratic Capitalism*. Amsterdam: IEA.

[17] There are several attempts to reframe the encounter with social sciences – but also to re-assess "secularisation" theory. For example, see Spalek and Imtoual, *Religion, Spirituality* and Grace Davie (2007) *The Sociology of Religion*. Thousand Oaks: Sage. Also, Gareth Morgan (1997) *Images of Organisation*. Thousand Oaks, CA: Sage.

striking for us that, at the outset, many Anglican Bishops reported that the Church of England's contribution "had declined" or "was no longer significant," and how this was a source of "sadness" for them. In fact, in the sphere of social welfare and voluntary action we found the opposite to be the case.[18]

In contrast, the Catholic Bishops had invested a good deal of energy in expressing publicly their undying solidarity with "the stranger" and yet we found that Catholic action in the refugee field was patchy or poor (to say the least) and did not match Episcopal rhetoric by any means. For example, the diocese of one of the unsuccessful candidates for the Archbishopric of Westminster is a peak area of asylum seeker dispersal, and yet there has been no response at all from the local church despite media comment from the ordinary concerned.[19]

Perhaps more controversially the formal Catholic position on relationships and sexuality is well known. Nevertheless, in a recent further survey of 1000 Mass-going Catholics that I led we found upwards of 80% of those interviewed had life practices at variance with the Church's teaching. A majority expressed disagreement with the formal position (even when they did not know what it was!).[20]

Meanwhile, as the Catholic Bishops of England and Wales were lobbying Labour politicians over the "Catholic" position on homosexuality, Labour advisors had a government opinion poll that suggested English Catholics were out of step with their Bishops in this sphere of relationships, too.[21]

Even with seemingly "fundamentalist" terrorists such a multiplicity of layers can often be in play as an enthusiasm for modern film and video

---

[18] Workshop with Anglican Bishops. Subsequent findings in Francis Davis, Elizabeth Paulhus and Andrew Bradstock (2008) *Moral, But No Compass: Government, Church and the Future of Welfare*. Chelmsford: Matthew James.

[19] Jolanta Stankeviciute, Jenny Rossiter and Francis Davis (2008) *National Mapping of the Catholic Church's Work in Refugee, Migration and Asylum Rights*. Caritas Social Action/Von Hugel Institute.

[20] "Revealed: The Modern Catholic," in *The Tablet*, 19/26 July 2008, accessed March 2013: http://www.thetablet.co.uk/article/11733.

[21] Interview.

games or theatre clashes with other layers of awareness.[22] Recognition of the causes of political violence is key here.

It may seem trite to re-state it but Churches, and wider faith communities, influenced by competing pathways from modernity to post-modernity in fragmenting cultures, may share a written "vision," or even a self-description, which is out of kilter with the social reality within and around them. Linda Woodhead, writing in the Tablet, has called this the modern multiple layers of religious identity and meaning.

This can be addressed partly by the disputation that I have referred to above. Additionally, I want to suggest that, in truly discerning our place in local neighbourhoods, national polities and global societies even faith-based institutions that would seek to emphasise their orientation, or disciplinary priority, as "theological"[23] need to return to empirical research. In the 2009 study referred to above, my colleagues and I established that the UK state had no idea – nor intention of evidencing – the faith-based contribution to civic welfare despite claiming a coherent "faith and social cohesion strategy" by which to guide all government departments, and the allocation of financial resources. The Churches, and especially the Catholic Church advised by eminent theologians, had not even noticed.[24]

In a climate of "evidence based policy making"[25] our discovery of the lack of research in faith-based areas revealed the state-Christian institution conversation to be grounded in policy-making sand. Conversely, the government opinion poll referred to above suggested that sometimes "outsiders" know more about us than we (or at least some Christian leaders) dare admit to ourselves. Meanwhile, the Muslim community was being over-researched not least by using theologians rather than those rooted in the social sciences. The Prevent programme

---

[22] See Richard English (1999) *Ernie O'Malley: IRA Intellectual*. Oxford: OUP, and Richard English (2010) *Terrorism: How To Respond*. Oxford: OUP.

[23] Ryan Topping, "St Augustine, Liberalism and The Defence of Liberal Education," in *New Blackfriars*, Vol. 89, No. 1024, 2008.

[24] In the UK the Secretary of State for Communities and Local Government has "lead" responsibility on these matters.

[25] Harsh organisational conflicts were described by those advising the Bishops as "the NHS being the metaphor of the Good Samaritan" while the scale and purpose of the Christian voluntary sector had been under intense scrutiny during the passage of the UK 2006 Charity Act but had not registered in the core activity of the Bishops' Conference Secretariat.

was a conservative Christian theological response to political radicalisation and violence that skipped most of what social policy and sociological researchers of any eminence had written in such fields.

More crucially still, if the Churches (in this case) could not provide – nor value – evidence about themselves either then might this not also suggest that their own planning for catechesis must be as unrooted as the state's policy judgements? Political witness, for example, would consequently be at risk of being muddled despite exhortation towards "social teaching," "political theology" or even generous secondments of higher education staff to ecclesiastical commissions to draft innumerable statements on the "ethics of society."[26]

While we renew our conversations about social enterprise, then, we also need to renew the means by which we discern the patterns of the "places" and networks that we serve. This could also help us be more honest about the potential – and limits – of our contribution.

In preparing such clarifications we may, if my interviewees are to be believed, likely discover that because of a "kleptocratic" state structure, destroyed civic sphere, or extreme consumerism we cannot any longer assume a rich "common good" as a starting point for our efforts. Instead, we may have to turn to faith communities as places of relevant institutional renewal in the new dark ages which are upon us.[27]

---

[26] From a theological distance – and many episcopal observations – Europe may look uniformly secular (but with Christian legacies) and yet most of the pioneering sociological studies in the region suggest a huge variety of secularisms at play that merit attention. In the UK we have been described as "believing without belonging" as while 71% of our citizens say they believe in a Christian God a little under 10% of them find their way to church. This has been contrasted with a North European tendency to "belong without believing," leading some to suggest that religion in the UK is a "half way" case between the religiosity of the US and the barren lands of Scandinavia. However, these judgments may again be affected by the structure and culture of the local state and its policy making habits. It is ironic that, despite an explicit commitment to *laïcité*, the French state is one of those most interested, at the policy level, in establishing which are the "acceptable" religious voices in society. Meanwhile, I have argued elsewhere that the state's creation of social partnership councils, or "structured dialogue," in Europe can have more influence on theological authenticity – even of minority Christian communities – than any number of worthy papers, episcopal utterances, church-going numbers or levels of Christian presence in national cabinets.

[27] I am consciously using imagery here from Alasdair Macintyre (2001) *After Virtue: A Study in Moral Theory*. London: Duckworth.

A question remains, however, as to what such an "institutional renewal" would look like. It is to this question that I now turn.

Ideas, institutions and the public realm

Assessments of the rise of the New Right as a force to convert minds, hearts and cultures in the last century repeatedly note the profound seriousness with which that movement used organisations and institutions as vehicles to carry civic outlooks, cultural aspirations and policy habits.[28]   Dionne even suggests that in the US neo-conservative case such a concern with right thinking about ideas and institutions arose from lessons learnt by neo-conservatives during youthful sallies into the New Left.[29]

Consequently, in a reversal of the "New Left" allegation that elite forces in society set out to "capture" the state for their own purposes,[30] the cultural New Right sought to take control of school boards, state level bodies and certain private and charitable entities. Just as friars invented the new institutional form of the mendicant preaching order to reach unchurched urban centres, so also did the New Right invent its own institutions to carry its principles, habits and vision into the public square.

New Right think tanks have been among the most entrepreneurial entities on the planet, working together to support common goals and continuing to reach out with an astounding focus: they share a commitment to the development of recognisable and "high quality" brands, and they identify clear "arenas" or "publics" with whom they wish to communicate. They develop, moreover, a deep knowledge of the patterns of life – and decision making – of those within these "arenas." Although they have a "clear line," such think tanks are explicitly independent, developing particular gifts for transcending traditional

---

[28] In this section I am drawing throughout on Raymond Plant and Kenneth Hoover (1991) *Conservative Capitalism in Britain and the US – A Critical Appraisal*. Oxford: Routledge; Andrew Denham (1996) *Think Tanks of the New Right*. Sudbury, MA: Dartmouth; Diane Stone and Andrew Denham (2004) *Think Tank Traditions: Policy Analysis Across Nations*. Manchester: Manchester University Press, and interviews at various think tanks in Washington DC by the author (2005).
[29] Eugene Dionne (2004) *Why Americans Hate Politics*. London: Simon and Schuster.
[30] Ramesh Mishra (1977) *Society and Social Policy*. London: Macmillan.

boundaries between the private, public and voluntary sectors in order to maximise their personal networks and institutional impact on cultures.

To assist in all of this the neo-conservative movements also gathered around them new philanthropic resources. This included some foundations specifically focused on backing those who seek to launch fresh New Right institutions in Eastern Europe and Asia especially.[31]

In Rome, the Acton Institute has set itself the task of "converting" young seminarians, at Santa Croce and Gregorian universities to name but two, while at Washington DC's Heritage Foundation "network coordinators" support ideological allies across the country, and match new donors with intellectual entrepreneurs wanting to establish fresh conservative think tanks.[32] Their approaches to dissemination, and highly targeted publication of research findings, can move public and private policy and culture at speed. It is an approach now being emulated by a new wave of "think" and "do" tanks on the moderate UK left,[33] and it is thus no wonder that, as Giddens has argued, neo-liberalism was, at least until the current liquidity crisis for banks, the only "revolutionary" ideology on the planet.[34]

The "successes" of the New Right are significant for reflection on faith-based actions because they locate ideas distribution in very specific settings (despite much normative core content) and link them to new "legs" by which to journey, namely niche networks within the full range of dominant institutions between state, business and civil society.

In the faith-based setting, certain communities may sometimes be at risk of giving inadequate attention to such institutional variety and focus. Especially in episcopal denominations in Christianity, huge claims can be made about the potential of a "congregation," but when they begin new ventures these huge claims actually cause the congregation to start out with a sense of powerlessness. This can happen in the Muslim community, too, when social work and health professionals assume that all mosques have the organisational capacity of the East London Muslim Centre, only to discover that prayer may be taking place on a Friday in a

---

[31] For example, The Atlas Foundation.
[32] Interview at Heritage Foundation, Dec 2004, and Acton Institute, 2008.
[33] See, for example, www.youngfoundation.org and its global network.
[34] Anthony Giddens (2004) *Beyond Left and Right: The Future of Radical Politics*. Cambridge: Polity Press.

borrowed room, or a mosque which is a small terraced house.[35] Vision is not matched to the capacity of institutional vehicles.

In turn, this may hinder potential to distribute ideas – our words – and the embedding of habits that might arise from them. Dreams become detached from the means to sustain them, or fall back on existing structures while still claiming "newness." Alternatively, "statements" or "resolutions" are released without a clear understanding of the "publics" to be addressed.[36] And so "advocacy" makes people of faith feel better without finding a letterbox through which to pass to actually change the system around them.

For example, an established church (and ours has) may seek out "fresh expressions" of mission[37] which, despite much fanfare to the contrary, mirror very closely the current geographical forms of mission work which have emerged in response to previous patterns of social and pastoral need. Likewise, in terrains where denominations have seen themselves as a "national" (albeit not established) church, the Christian reflex may be to sustain "the old" at great cost to that which is emerging; rather like a monopoly objecting to incursions from innovative small businesses. The authentic alternative is not, however, to suggest an unreflective escape but to find new ways to start again.

My contention is that the contexts in which the religious communities find themselves are constantly changing, and it is unlikely that new wine will be held by old wineskins. Moreover, as institutional pressures arise on the religious communities in general and the churches in particular, these groups can become the depository of all of the hopes of leaderships as they struggle to make sense of a difficult new missionary terrain.[38]

As hopes multiply, innumerable images of the faith-based social enterprise and innovation go with them. When those discourses run back

---

[35] Interview 2009.

[36] See the sections on "Exit, Voice and Loyalty" in Davis, Paulhus and Bradstock, *Moral, But No Compass.*

[37] The "Fresh Expressions" initiatives of Dioceses of the Church of England that we visited as part of *Moral, But No Compass* were "all local … all seeking to rebuild a local church" and had much in common with earlier attempts by the Methodist Urban Theology Unit (www.utusheffield.org.uk) to make churches more community focused.

[38] "We cannot replace families, catechesis … or turn round a whole society" says one interviewee educational institution head, 2008.

into the communities concerned, the likelihood of strategic drift increases as metaphor is piled upon metaphor to defend an ever more inclusive brief.

In seeking to re-ground our common mission, then, we need not only to encourage common disputation and to root these debates in new social research about the role of faith in the society of today. Like the New Right, we also need common and compelling institutions and practical projects which mark out our niches and demonstrate our energy. Our new talk and fresh research could then be the basis of renewal and re-invention – not maintenance. It could be the basis of energetic ideas, institutions and impacts as strategic as the New Right but with a much deeper hope on offer for the dark ages in which new lights must shine.

Religious communities as social silicon valleys

St John's College with Cranmer Hall, in the University of Durham,[39] can lay claim (with justice) to being the founding home of the UK Fairtrade Movement: from within its walls emerged Tearcraft, which subsequently divided to give birth to Traidcraft, which, in turn, has grown to become the closest thing to an ecumenical UK household name. At around the same time the college was educating others who would go on to make outstanding national contributions in the field of social entrepreneurship.[40]

Theologically, such an interlocking set of developments might have one description, but this may run the risk failing to recognise the attributes of religious institutions which enable them to renew their ability to, at their best, innovate. While the Fairtrade cause was being launched in Durham, in other parts of the UK the anti-homelessness movement was growing out of faith-led responses to social need. It culminated in the vital religious contribution to the first ever British legislation to protect vulnerable homeless people.[41] Since then, the Jubilee Debt campaign emerged out of an evangelical seminar at Keele University, while the

---

[39] See www.dur.ac.uk/st-johns.college/durham.ac.uk.

[40] For example, Rev Brian Strevens founded the UK social enterprise of the year, The SCA Group; and Rev Chris Beales (who went also to found the Inner Cities Religious Council under Mrs Thatcher's government) runs pioneering social enterprises generating revenues for Afghanistan.

[41] The 1977 Housing (Homeless Persons) Act was taken through parliament by Stephen Ross MP with key advice from church-based groups.

Make Poverty History campaign has been nurtured by faith groups. London Citizens, moreover, would never have emerged without collaboration across Jewish, Muslim and trade union as well as Christian entities, and even the committedly "secular" Amnesty International has its origins in liberal religion, with some describing the organisation as a form of "religionless" faith.[42]

What has changed since those pioneering days is that, on the one hand, we have learned a good deal about the effects of "clustering" on the potential success of new enterprises, while, on the other, a more structured movement for "social innovation" has emerged on the global stage.[43] It is in relation to this realm of enquiry and action that I want to propose a response to the crying need for new institutions in which we might embed habits of the heart (by which I mean those practices which we inculcate as at the centre of our lives and communities).

"Social Innovation" refers to new strategies, concepts, ideas and organisations that meet social and spiritual needs of all kinds – from working conditions and education to community development and health. They also extend and strengthen civil society.

Social innovation can take place within and between each of the public, private and voluntary sectors and can sometimes be seen as a process (e.g. open source technologies) or as a way of addressing a social problem (e.g. micro-finance).

As such, this is not a simplistic call for an MBA programme with a bit more "sustainability" in its non-profit track. Perhaps even more crucially, it is not an advocacy for a traditional extension of "service learning" programmes, nor stand-alone technology or enterprise accelerators.

---

[42] Stephen Hopgood (2006) *Keepers of the Flame: Understanding Amnesty International*. Ithaca, NY: Cornell.

[43] See www.youngfoundation.org.uk. Also, http://www.gsb.stanford.edu/csi/, www.socialinnovationexchange.org and the Skoll Centre For Social Enterprise at Said Business School, Oxford. For a more passionate Christian take, see Alison Elliott (2006) "The Spirit Of Social Innovation," a lecture for the International Futures Forum at the Scottish Parliament (www.internationalfuturesforum.com/iff-publications.php). Elliott is the former Moderator of the Church of Scotland and is based currently at New College, Edinburgh University.

Important though all of those strategies are my argument is that we have not sought to reflect adequately on sources of faith-based social innovation. In faith-based networks this has robbed us of the opportunity to develop as many common projects as we might have done.[44] In society, it has reduced recognition of what we contribute.[45]

There are now opportunities to develop physical and virtual faith-based social innovation parks – or what I have called elsewhere "social silicon valleys."[46] These would be "hubs" around which the rethinking of social and civic renewal can be grounded.

"Social silicon valleys" would go further than the more utilitarian models that surround us: first, there would be much more systematic learning about how to support social innovation from a faith base, and this would build on increasingly sophisticated understandings of social entrepreneurship, enterprise and the impact of mission innovation.

Second, such "valleys" would seek to proliferate better ways to spot, create, incubate and scale up good ideas, people and methods so that they can be embedded in existing, new and – crucially – scalable institutions.

Thirdly, they would seek to garner new sources (and methods) of support to make such a potential deliverable.

Although we think about religions in metaphors all the time, I know that some will only be able to imagine what such a "knowledge transfer" or "innovation explosion" strategy would look like if I offer concrete examples. So what might set our "social silicon valleys" apart?

First, they would be led by those with direct access to senior management. Such a positioning would locate the mission of the "valley" at the heart of the institution and across all departments.[47] I will return to this matter in a later section. Faith-based parliamentarians could be key, here.

---

[44] Even in the USA adequate provision for members of Religious Orders did not come from "within" but from the uncomfortable questions of leading Catholic foundations "without." See Mary Oates (1995) *The Catholic Philanthropic Tradition in America*. Bloomington, IN: Indiana University Press.

[45] A key argument of Davis, Paulhus and Bradstock, *Moral, But No Compass*.

[46] Geoff Mulgan et al. (2006) *Social Silicon Valleys*. Young Foundation/British Council.

[47] Interview, Southampton University Health Innovation Unit, 2008.

Second, the "valleys" would see themselves as effervescing centres of faith-based social enterprise, innovation and creativity and would look to attract energetic talent to them from across the region – and the planet. This is not to minimise the insights of spirituality and religious rationality. However, our "valleys" would be looking to launch new modes of action that can be internationalised or adopted by others for roll out on a larger scale. Such things may indeed happen "informally" or "by the grace of God" in many local places but the "social silicon valley" would structure them, back them and replicate them. It would help them to bypass some of the institutional nightmares that have been common even to clearly holy causes.[48] It would introduce them to the global Christian – and/or faith – community (and beyond).

Moreover, "social silicon valleys" would have a particular brief to contribute to the renewal of market relationships and voluntary- and public-sector innovation in these trying times. Despite condemnations in some "rational" economic quarters, there is still scope to bring together principle-driven family entrepreneurs, firms from the "Mutual top 300" and unique business forms, such as the international ecumenical movement Focolare's "Economy of Communion," in shared physical – and virtual – spaces. There they could develop new institutions and learn from the best social entrepreneurs in the world. The first target for the evidence gathering – to support an open source faith-based international social innovation network – would be the most successful models of practice developed by the faith communities globally. After all, religious communities run more educational and social welfare institutions than they do parishes![49]

As new horizons are broken open, fresh forms of funding would be needed to pump prime and help scale the "valley's" contribution. While some resources may flow from traditional giving, a new pooling of effort would give "social silicon valleys" a regional network, national links and international sources of funds.

---

[48] The "constitutionalism" of the Dominicans as a contrast to the fragmentation of the Franciscans being a case in point. Even the anti-homelessness movement praised earlier encountered a series of striking "splits" as it grew from roots in the Society of St. Dismas in Southampton.

[49] Brian Froehle and Mary Gautier (2003) *Global Catholicism: Portrait of a World Church*. Maryknoll, NY: Orbis.

These might include the younger generation of faith-based, high-net-worth individuals and family foundation members. They are (very often) exasperated by the lack of innovation shown by faith leaderships – not to mention the obsession with fixed assets! These young risk takers would be particularly attracted because it would be demonstrating a faith-based network at the front end of the innovation curve rather than playing "catch up."[50] Either way, a skill of the institution would be to devise new packages of funding across the public, private, religious and philanthropic sectors to develop the "social silicon valleys."

Combined, these new collaborations could also add a fresh focus to religious volunteering. They could be significantly channeled in the direction of helping the launch stages of new initiatives with *pro bono* skills and social networks.

Very concretely, then, a "social silicon valley" located in, or launched from, a faith-based institution should not simply debate the demise of "education," the collapse of "finance" or the "decline of virtue" in silos. It would seek less to take on the woes of the faith-based theological task and more to be a locus of institutional renewal of both faith-based communities and society. In essence, it would become a social and religious research and development centre that would enable us to scatter networked, innovative and prophetic institutional fragments across a culture that needs saving.[51]

To concretise such "communities of character" even more they could look like, for example, a Zweite Sparkasse, a Cristo Rey/Studio School, the Cathedral Innovation Centre or the Economy of Communion.

Zweite Sparkasse[52]

Die Zweite Sparkasse was launched in 2006 in a partnership between Erste Bank in Vienna and Caritas Austria. It is a "bank for the

---

[50] Based on interviews with philanthropists (2008) and the explicit comment from the Church of England Education Board that the "conundrum is the lack of compelling projects rather than a shortage of resources" (2008). See also studies in changing attitudes to Christian family philanthropy published by Foundations and Donors Interested in Catholic Activities, www.fadica.org.

[51] I take this phrase from the title of Dudley Plunkett (2007) *Saving Secular Society*. Stoke on Trent: Alive Publications.

[52] See also: www.guardian.co.uk/commentisfree/belief/2009/feb/02/religion-catholicism, accessed March 2013.

unbankable" and spread quickly to Austria's regions. It is staffed wholly by volunteers from the banking sector who gain client referrals because the churches' routes to local neighbourhoods and communities facing poverty are so strong. This experience could be repeated in, for example, the UK, where in urban priority areas clergy are often the only "professionals" that actually live locally, and where so many local churches have become outlets for the national Post Office.

Services offered by this new social bank include a basic account, a bank card, an investment account with interest and an optional building loan contract. In cooperation with a local insurance provider, cover is also available at a discounted cost. New customers are automatically able to access free legal advice on a quarterly basis. Crucially, the credit account is not a stand-alone product aimed at people in personal distress but forms part of a multi-faceted package of counselling and support services provided by welfare organisations and the churches. In the UK such support might prove timely as incapacity benefit is reined in and unemployment increases dramatically.

Fascinatingly, the model is now being extended to Romania where pyramid selling scandals had damaged the banks even before the current crisis. Here, in rural areas, the Erste Foundation is testing the use of mobile phone technology as a replacement for an excessively costly branch structure. This mirrors the use, in Ireland, of "pay as you go" cards to help African migrants send remittances home to their families.[53]

Cathedral Innovation Centre (CIC)

Founded in Portsmouth in 2011, the CIC was significantly inspired by the Jewish Innovation Hub established by the Pears Foundation in North London.

Portsmouth Anglican Cathedral made available some under-used office space and a new co-operative legal entity was registered with the Financial Services Authority. The CIC was then awarded "catalyst" status by the Royal Society of Arts. Those seeking to launch a new firm, social venture or entrepreneurial response to pressing need are able to become members of the CIC, where they receive a tailor-made package

---

[53] Francis Davis, "Migrating Money," in *The Tablet*, 27 Jan, 2007.

of finance, cheap to discounted office space, a mentor recruited from the RSA, local businesses and congregations and pooled marketing support. In 2013 a community share flotation will be launched to raise £150,000 of funding under the government's SEED funding scheme, which attracts 50% income tax relief for those who pay tax.

Before being launched, the CIC is full, has a waiting list and has now been offered buildings across the country to replicate its model. For a total cost of £9000 it has opened 14 start-up desks (while a government-backed equivalent locally is still working its way through £2 million).

Cristo Rey/Studio Schools[54]

Cristo Rey schools originated in US inner-city areas as a response to the cost of a faith-based education in a setting where the state will not fund Church schools, and also as a means to combat teenage truancy.

Students attend on four days a week for vocational classes grounded in a strong faith ethos, and on the fifth day – still part of their school week – they work one fifth of a real job in a company which has committed to be a "corporate partner."

The vocational skills are meaningful to the students, while the "real job" gives them references and social networks from organisations and addresses outside their stereotyped neighbourhoods. Moreover, the pay they receive makes their education 65% self funding and the sense of responsibility this conveys has slashed truancy rates.

When the UK government heard about Cristo Rey Schools they copied it directly, including the possibility to develop new "Studio Schools" in a new education act.

Economy of Communion (EOC)

Inspired by Chiara Lubich, "Economy of Communion" seeks to add a more "human dimension" into the marketplace. EOC businesses work in networks or come together in their own business parks. They commit to sharing a tithe of profits with community initiatives and reaching out in other ways.

---

[54] Francis Davis, "The Government Borrows Another Great Catholic Idea," in *Catholic Herald*, 23 Nov, 2007.

While this may smack of idealism thus far, over the last ten years some 750 businesses in more than 30 countries have joined the movement.

Most are small to medium businesses with a turnover of less than 20 million dollars annually. In some parts of Europe, and in South America, the EOC businesses have formed a network and co-operate in publishing promotional material. More than 200 EOC businesses are in South America and 300 in Europe. Some 100 are focused on agriculture, some 300 in the service sector and the rest in manufacturing and industry. In 1997, 23 German business people established an EOC Merchant Bank, dedicated to the development of EOC businesses in Eastern Europe, the Middle East and other parts of the world.

Value, values and civic value

Finally, I want to turn to the question of "measurement." It is, of course, when we address questions of "demonstrable" value in education, and especially faith-based education, that we can run into the deepest problems of terminology that I referred to at the outset.[55] However, I want to suggest here that the avoidance of "measurement" that some in the religious communities (and especially the Churches) advocate is in fact a flight from reason and justice, and is likely to further complicate our relationships with the "secular" – and, increasingly, charitable donor – sphere.

In the UK, a number of religious bodies have withdrawn from academic "league tables," objecting that they do not "represent the fullness of education of the whole person."[56] Others have complained – having entered students who have "not done so well" – that "targets measure the wrong thing."[57] In some cases, measurement in general has been condemned as mere "positivism."[58] These stances seem inadequate on at least three grounds.

---

[55] And yet respondents in Christian organisations often talk of a "value added" in a faith organisation that is absent from their "secular" counterparts.
[56] Stonyhurst College in the period 2003-05 is a case in point.
[57] A repeated reservation among interviewed Catholic teachers in our sample.
[58] Archbishop Vincent Nichols, Chairman of the Catholic Education Services, has expressed this view.

First, there is a moral communication issue: we may seek to articulate an "idea of the common good," which all people of reason may espouse, but at the very moment that people of "good will" ask for evidence of such warm intentions the religious person often retreats too readily into the unknowability of all that they do. If it is a "common" good, can it not be commonly quantified without becoming subsumed into target-setting bureaucracy?

Second, the religious tendency to conflate "measurement," "utilitarian immorality" and "market values" is intellectually dishonest. Our colleagues should be able to remind us that the history of accounting,[59] along with the best of current developments in economics, offers us alternative vistas.

For example, current management accounting and audit methods are the product of negotiation, historical circumstance and the power of professions, not tablets of stone uncritically binding on all institutions. Additionally, for all of its weaknesses in relation to population, "Green" economics is developing new means by which to factor "future generations," "qualities of life" and other seeming intangibles into the assessment of "value."[60] This is without mentioning the work of Mark Moore on "public value," and others on "blended value" and the "social return on investment."[61]

Instead of being caught in the wider ecclesial culture of complaint, Christian universities need to be at the forefront of conversations about who, what and how to "measure": we need to develop our own reasonable and reasoned matrices of value – let us call them "civic value."

One of the advantages of the "social silicon valley" model is that it allows "metrics" development to become one of the integrated but experimental features of the creation of new social institutions and innovations in which Christian principles are embedded. The "valley"

---

[59] Keith Hoskin (2005) "Leading or Horses: History and Management," lecture at Warwick University. See also, http://www.wbs.ac.uk/faculty/members/keith/hoskin.
[60] See, for example, Partha Dasgupta (2001) *Human Well-Being and the Natural Environment.* Oxford: Oxford University Press
[61] Mark Moore (1995) Creating Public Value: Strategic Management in Government. Cambridge, MA: Harvard University Press. See also Jed Emerson's work on www.blendedvalue.org and for social return on investment (SROI) see www.neweconomics.org.

becomes the accounting and economic laboratory in which new frameworks may be devised. And, once again, this presents the opportunity for rich inter-disciplinary conversation, common collaboration and witness in the public sphere.

Conclusion

In this paper I have sought to begin to tease out a case for new strategies of "knowledge transfer" on the part of Christian institutions.

Influenced mostly by the European context, I suggested that we live in an increasingly fragmented culture – a new dark age. When such fragmentation is mixed with a lack of nuanced evidence on the part of the state and religious communities, these communities risk becoming fragmented themselves. They are also at risk of becoming depositories of excessive hopes or concerns.

In pursuit of a clearer identity I suggested that it is in a return to the rapidly-evolving social sciences that much hope could be found – even by institutions that consider theology or religious reflection to have prior (or superior) disciplinary standing.

In order to renew a reasonable understanding of ourselves I proposed a conscious culture of institutional disputation combined with new evidence gathering. I also proposed the development of new common projects, not least of which would be a series of "social silicon valleys." These "valleys" would be structured centres where new institutions for dark times could be invented and scaled.

As hubs of energy they could not save a national or established church, or protect a community from anti-Semitism or Islamophobia, but they could become the bases from which might emerge new institutions linking ideas, community and impact to support positive action. By combining disputation, common talk, shared research and common social risk taking we would seek to make knowledge transfer a habit of the heart. In so doing we may just give rise to some hope in the midst of the enduring economic crisis upon us.